Emilia Pardo Bazán

Statue of Emilia Pardo Bazán, in the Gardens of Méndez Núñez, La Coruña.
Artist: Lorenzo Coullaut Valera. Photo by Robert M. Fedorchek.

Emilia Pardo Bazán

"The White Horse" and Other Stories

Translated from the Spanish by
Robert M. Fedorchek

Lewisburg
Bucknell University Press
London and Toronto: Associated University Presses

English translation © 1993 by Robert M. Fedorchek

Associated University Presses
440 Forsgate Drive
Cranbury, NJ 08512

Associated University Presses
25 Sicilian Avenue
London WC1A 2QH, England

Associated University Presses
P.O. Box 338, Port Credit
Mississauga, Ontario
Canada L5G 4L8

Library of Congress Cataloging-in-Publication Data

Pardo Bazán, Emilia, condesa de, 1852–1921.
    "The white horse" and other stories / Emilia Pardo Bazán ;
translated from the Spanish by Robert M. Fedorchek.
        p.   cm.
    Includes bibliographical references.
    ISBN 0-8387-5258-6 (alk. paper)
    1. Pardo Bazán, Emilia, condesa de, 1852–1921—Translations into
English.   I. Title.
PQ6629.A7A24   1993
863'.5—dc20
                                                        92-54944
                                                        CIP

PRINTED IN THE UNITED STATES OF AMERICA

Mi inolvidable padre [My unforgettable father] was how Emilia Pardo Bazán referred to her father when he died. Mine, John Fedorchek, passed away while I was at work on this translation and I dedicate it to his memory, for he too shall be *inolvidable*.

Contents

Translator's Foreword

Several days after Emilia Pardo Bazán's death on 12 May 1921, her longtime friend Miguel de Unamuno paid tribute to her in a newspaper article, speaking of her "admirable industry" and "unquenchable curiosity."[1] The first characterization can be viewed as an understatement, a muted reference aimed at a Spanish readership familiar with her writings and life, for "admirable industry" is scarcely sufficient to describe Pardo Bazán's *oeuvre*; this singular writer, one of the most extraordinary figures in all of Spanish literary history, was a (youthful) poet, critic, novelist, journalist, short story writer, polemicist, hagiographer, correspondent, (frustrated) dramatist, lecturer, essayist, translator, and social and political commentator. The second characterization, "unquenchable curiosity," is more than a trait; it is a definition of her makeup, for she lived life to such a full extent that an accounting, albeit superficial, of her activities has an air of the unreal about it. Pardo Bazán was a writer, an intellectual, an autodidact, and a polyglot; she was an indefatigable traveler, wife (at age sixteen), mother (of three children), amateur botanist, publisher (Library for Women), founder and president of the Galician Folklore Society, (government-appointed) adviser on public education, president of the literary section of the Athenaeum of Madrid, (first woman) professor of contemporary Romance literatures at the Central University of Madrid, and an ardent feminist and champion of equality for women (at a time when equal rights attracted little support from either sex in Spain). She was sympathetic to Carlism; she was a devout Catholic and an aristocrat who enjoyed nobility's many privileges; and she found time to collect recipes and publish a book entitled *Modern Spanish Cuisine.*

---

1. Carmen Bravo Villasante, *Vida y obra de Emilia Pardo Bazán* (Madrid: Editorial Magisterio Español, 1973), p. 308.

9

An admired novelist and a respected critic, Emilia Pardo Bazán is also considered, by virtually all scholars and students of Spanish literature, one of nineteenth-century Spain's foremost short story writers. Others (Leopoldo Alas) can be more profound and some (Pedro Antonio de Alarcón and Armando Palacio Valdés) are considerably more gifted with a sense of humor, but few of her Spanish contemporaries have her range and none her volume. The critic Juan Paredes Núñez has been able to locate the staggering number of 580 stories, and states that even this figure is not definitive inasmuch as Pardo Bazán published not only in Spain, but also in numerous foreign newspapers and magazines.[2]

If Nathaniel Hawthorne is an American short story writer who best depicts New England, and Guy de Maupassant a French short story writer who best depicts Normandy, then Doña Emilia Pardo Bazán is to be seen as a Spanish short story writer who best depicts her home region of Galicia. Situated in the northwestern corner of Spain, Galicia saw itself in the nineteenth century as remote, isolated from the central government, and cut off from Castile by forbidding mountains. It was and is the garden of Spain, a lush, verdant land of valleys and woods, fields and dairy farms, streams and estuaries; a land blessed with the bounty of the ocean, which surrounds it from Vigo in the southwest to Ribadeo in the northeast. Galicia is a land steeped in history: La Coruña, the capital city where Pardo Bazán was born in 1851, the port of departure for emigrants to the New World; Santiago de Compostela, the ageless, universal city of pilgrimage; Orense, ancient city of gold (oro) panned from the River Sil; Lugo, a Roman city surrounded by ancient walls; Pontevedra, at the head of an inland bay. It is the land of hórreos (elevated rectangular granaries set on stone pillars) and pazos (manor houses of the gentry), of peasants who squeeze a living from the earth; it is the land where Pardo Bazán usually spent three or four months of the year, principally at her pazo in Meirás, not far from La Coruña; it is a land rich in customs and Catholic tradition, with a language more like Portuguese than Castilian.

Doña Emilia Pardo Bazán, the cosmopolite, the aristocrat, the

2. *Emilia Pardo Bazán, Cuentos*, ed. Juan Paredes Núñez (Madrid: Taurus, 1985), p. 42.

socialite who resided most of her life in Madrid, was inextricably bound to the Galicia of her childhood and adolescence, but unlike her sister writer, the poet Rosalía de Castro, she chose Castilian, that is, Spanish, rather than Galician as her linguistic medium. Was she announcing to Spain that she was a regionalist but not a separatist (as many Galicians were, and are)? Did she wish to find a greater audience? Was she simply more "at home" in Castilian? We may never know what the choice did mean, but perhaps we can hazard guessing what it did not mean—a rejection of her roots. Quite the opposite: her love and knowledge of Galicia was central to her grasp of the universal, the heritage that equipped her to explore the gamut of human responses, for like all great writers her uniqueness—the "Galicianness" inseparable from her "Spanishness"—was her understanding of the land and people that nurtured her in order to represent the commonality of mankind.

Interested as she was in the reality around her, Pardo Bazán often found the subject matter of her stories in the mysteries and vicissitudes of life. Some tales are fictional accounts of actual occurrences or people ("The Pardon," "A Galician Mother," "The Lady Bandit"); others are a defense of women subjugated by a double standard ("The Guilty Woman," "The Faithful Fiancée"); a number focus on the figure of the rural priest ("A Descendant of the Cid," "Don Carmelo's Salvation"); one is highly symbolic ("The White Horse") and qualifies Pardo Bazán as the godmother of the Generation of 98, the group of writers who exhorted Spain to rid itself of inertia, apathy and fixation on past glories in order to begin anew; several are like contemporary tales of suspense ("The Cuff Link," "The White Hair"); many reveal keen psychological insight ("The Torn Lace," "The Substitute," "Scissors," "The Nurse," "Rescue"); and her themes are fear, love, hatred, forgiveness, cruelty, poverty, necrophilia, repentance, homesickness, madness, and so on—that is, naked reality, bitter reality, and very often an ugly, vicious reality.

It can be said that Pardo Bazán's realities led her to a morbid realism, that her stories frequently highlight the perverse, the wicked, the cruel; it can also be said that many of her stories are punctuated with naturalistic detail or emphasis ("The Gravedig-

ger," "Consolation"), not surprising in a writer who created a
sensation in Spain when she published The Burning Question
(1882-83), an introduction to and critical commentary on Zola's
theories that earned her numerous enemies (who believed that
she espoused in their entirety the French novelist's ideas) and
precipitated the separation from her husband. Are we to conclude that she had a proclivity for blood, torture, cruelty, depravity, desecration, misery, and death? No, but as Carmen Bravo
Villasante suggests, there is a possible explanation for her attraction to the dark side of life: Francisco de Goya, the celebrated
painter of the court of Carlos IV. In 1901 Pardo Bazán gave a
lecture at the Fine Arts Center of Madrid entitled "Goya and
Spanish Spontaneity." After remarking that some of the Iberian
tendencies seen in his work are cruelty, bloodthirstiness, ferocity,
and heroism conveyed through jarring contrasts of chiaroscuro,
she singled out his etchings: "Monstrosity, insanity, brutality, violent dementia, perversity, torture, and black magic tempt and
seduce him as an artist, even though he condemns all of it in
verbal lashings that accompany the drawings as commentary."[3]
If, like Goya, she was drawn to the gruesome in order to come to
grips with it, she also, like Goya, condemned it. Representation
of evil is not acceptance of it, much less approval. There can be
little doubt of the affinity, indeed, parallel, between the two great
Spaniards.

One of the indisputable giants of the nineteenth-century short
story is Guy de Maupassant. Pardo Bazán met him (along with
Daudet and Zola) in France and considered the author of "The
Horla" the master of short story writers. Although he influenced
her, most notably in psychological inquiry and careful attention
to realistic detail, Pardo Bazán put her own stamp on her stories
and developed a style *sui generis*, the most striking feature of
which is brevity. The *short* of the English term "short story" suits
her to a tee and describes admirably her tales. Rarely did she
write stories of the length of "Ball of Fat" (she would have called
them short novels or novellas); the vast majority average six or
seven pages, and one included here, "Soft-Boiled Eggs," is a mere
two pages.

---

3. Bravo Villasante, p. 253.

The essence of her approach is to engage the reader as quickly as possible, certainly in the first paragraph, frequently in the first few sentences. Some aspect of a character or an episode is brought to light and the story unfolds rapidly. There are third-person narratives in which the author occasionally injects herself or her point of view; others are presented wholly in the first person, a few by the omniscient narrator, some by the "players." From time to time another technique used by Pardo Bazán is to have someone tell the story to her, and then as narrator she becomes the audience. When she is the disinterested or omniscient narrator, Pardo Bazán maintains distance from her sex to appear ... what? As strong and detached as a man? As worldly as a man? It is entirely possible that some of her graphic descriptions were intended to blunt accusations of softness (i.e., femininity) that would be associated, foolishly, with a woman writer. Men are just as capable of maudlin outbursts and descriptions that ooze with sentimentality (and conversely are capable of the back-biting associated with women, as proven by Leopoldo Alas and Armando Palacio Valdés, her contemporaries). But when the time came to represent the plight of women—in terms of natural, understandable sexual needs and intellectual acceptance—Pardo Bazán wrote as a woman to capture the anguish and inferior status of her Spanish sisters.

Doña Emilia Pardo Bazán reflected the reality around her as well as the reality that she lived. Should she be called the Spanish Maupassant or should Maupassant be called the French Pardo Bazán? Should she be called the Spanish Chekhov or should Chekhov be called the Russian Pardo Bazán? Or should we speak of Turguenev, Hoffmann, Machado de Assis, Poe, Crane, Eça de Queirós, James, and ... other nineteenth-century short story writers? In the end, such comparisons may be useful, if only to suggest that these writers have transcended their linguistic borders, that through translation their catholic and enduring vision has awakened human chords in a large part of the world.

*   *   *

Words and passages marked with an asterisk (*) in the text are explained in the Notes at the back of the book.

Acknowledgments

Emilia Pardo Bazán's short stories are so numerous and varied that it would be a formidable task indeed to tackle them without guidance. For the perspective that they afforded me I wish to cite the Spanish critics Mariano Baquero Goyanes (deceased), Carmen Bravo Villasante, Marina Mayoral, and Juan Paredes Núñez (to whom I am also greatly indebted for the Brobdingnagian feat of researching original dates of publication of Pardo Bazán's stories and providing me with a chronology); and the American critics Robert E. Osborne—my mentor who many years ago introduced me to the fascinating world of Pardo Bazán's short prose fiction—and Walter T. Pattison.

For generous and patient assistance in deciphering the numerous difficulties that I encountered in Pardo Bazán's lexical labyrinth, I am deeply grateful to Pedro S. Rivas Díaz and Consuelo García Devesa; and for reading and commenting on the manuscript at various stages, I thank—once again—Pedro and Consuelo, as well as Salvatore F. Bongiorno and Theresa L. Fedorchek.

I gladly acknowledge my debt to the Royal Galician Academy, Calle Tabernas, 11, La Coruña—in particular Don Constantino García González, Don Domingo García Sabell, and Don Juan Naya Pérez—for gracious permission to translate and publish the twenty-seven short stories in this volume.

The primary sources of the texts for this translation are the several volumes of Pardo Bazán's short stories published by V. Prieto y Compañía (Madrid) in the late 1890s and early 1900s and third edition of the *Complete Works* published by Aguilar (Madrid, 1973).

Emilia Pardo Bazán

Bust of Emilia Pardo Bazán, in the Emilia Pardo Bazán Museum, La Coruña. Artist: Antonio Moltó y Lluch. Photo by Robert M. Fedorchek. Courtesy, Emilia Pardo Bazán Museum.

Portrait of Emilia Pardo Bazán, in the Emilia Pardo Bazán Museum, La Coruña. Artist: Gustav Wertheimer. Photo by Robert M. Fedorchek. Courtesy, Emilia Pardo Bazán Museum.

Emilia Pardo Bazán's *pazo* (manor) and longtime summer residence in Meirás, near La Coruña. She married here on 10 July 1868 at the age of sixteen. Photo by Robert M. Fedorchek.

Emilia Pardo Bazán, as depicted on a Spanish postage stamp. Photo by Michael A. Micinilio.

The Pardon*

Of all the women who were washing clothes at Marineda's* public laundry, numb from the bitter cold of a March morning, Antonia the cleaning lady was the most stooped, the most
downtrodden, the one who wrung each piece with the least
drive, and the one who scrubbed with the least enthusiasm. From
time to time she interrupted her work and ran the back of her
hand over her reddened eyelids, trailing beads of water and soap
bubbles that looked like tears on her withered skin.

Antonia's washerwomen companions watched her sympathet-
ically, and every now and then, in the midst of loud conversations and arguments, there was a brief exchange in a low voice,
a dialogue punctuated by exclamations of amazement, indignation, and compassion. The entire laundry knew the cleaning
lady's troubles down to the smallest detail and found them a
source of unending commentary. Nobody was unaware that the
miserable creature, married to a young butcher, lived some years
back with her mother and husband in a quarter outside the city,
and that the family got along comfortably thanks to Antonia's
assiduous work and the money saved by the old woman in her
former occupation as secondhand dealer, peddler, and money-
lender. No one had forgotten either the gloomy afternoon that
the old woman was murdered, when they found, smashed into
smithereens, the lid of the large chest where she kept her savings
and certain gold earrings and hair charms. Nor had anyone lost
sight of the horror provoked in people by the news that the thief
and murderer was none other than Antonia's husband, as she
herself testified, adding that for some time the criminal had
lusted after his mother-in-law's money, with which he wished to
start a butcher shop of his very own. Nevertheless, the defendant
attempted to establish an alibi, availing himself of the testimony
of two or three drinking buddies, and he distorted the facts to
such an extent that, instead of going to the gallows, he got off

21

with twenty years' imprisonment. Public opinion was less indulgent than the law. In addition to the wife's testimony, there was one incontestable piece of evidence: the knife wound that killed the old woman—a clean, well-aimed blow struck from top to bottom, like those used in slaughtering pigs, delivered with a wide and very keen meat cleaver. As far as the people were concerned, there was no doubt that he should have been hanged. Antonia's fate began to instill holy terror when rumors spread that her husband had sworn to get even with her the day he was released for having denounced him. The poor creature was pregnant, and the murderer warned her that, upon his return, she was as good as dead.

When Antonia's son was born she was unable to nurse him, such was her weakness and emaciation and the frequency of the anxieties that had afflicted her since the crime. And because she couldn't afford to pay a wet nurse, the neighborhood women who had unweaned infants took turns breast-feeding her baby, who grew up sickly, suffering the effects of all his mother's agonies. When she had recovered somewhat, Antonia devoted herself zealously to her work, and although her cheeks always had the bluish pallor seen in people with heart trouble, she regained her quiet energy and gentle manner.

'Twenty years' imprisonment! In twenty years,' she thought to herself, 'he can die or I can die, and from now until then is a long time.'

The notion of natural death didn't frighten her, but just imagining that her husband would return filled her with horror. The solicitous neighbor women comforted her in vain, pointing out the remote hope that the evil killer might repent, reform, or, as they said, come back a changed man. Antonia would shake her head then, murmuring gloomily:

"That? Him? A changed man? Not unless God himself comes down from heaven to tear out his rotten heart and give him another."

And talking about the criminal would send a chill down her spine.

But there are, after all, many days in twenty years and time heals even the most painful wounds. Occasionally Antonia imagined that everything that had happened was a dream; or that the penitentiary's wide jaws, which had swallowed the culprit, would never disgorge him; or that the law, which in the end had exacted punishment for the first crime, would know how to prevent the second. The law! That moral entity, of which Antonia was beginning to form a confused, mysterious concept, was, to be sure, a terrible force, but a protective one, an iron hand that would sustain her on the brink of an abyss. So it was that her unbounded fears were joined by an indefinable trust, based above all on the time that had already elapsed and on the remainder of the sentence to be served.

How bizarre is the link between events!

Certainly the king wouldn't have believed, standing before the altar dressed as a captain general, with a profusion of chest decorations, and giving his hand to a princess,* that such a solemn act meant infinite grief to a poor cleaning woman in a distant provincial capital. When Antonia learned that her husband had been granted a pardon, she didn't utter a word; the neighbor women saw her sitting on the doorsill, her hands clasped together, her head drooping over her chest, while the little boy, raising his pitiful and sickly face, whined:

"Mother . . . Warm up the soup for me, for heaven's sake! I'm hungry!"

The bevy of kindly, cackling neighbor women surrounded Antonia. Several set about preparing the child's meal; others cheered the mother up as best they could. It was really foolish to get all upset like that! Mother of Mercy! You'd think that he would kill her as soon as he arrived! There was a government, thank God, and courts, and night watchmen; one could appeal to the constables, to the mayor . . .

"What mayor!" she said with a sullen expression and muffled tone of voice.

"Or to the governor, or the magistrate, or the police chief. It was necessary to go to a lawyer to see what provisions the law made . . ."

One robust young woman, married to a civil guard, volunteered to send her husband around "to scare the daylights" out of the villain; another, bold and swarthy, offered to stay every night and sleep in the cleaning woman's house. In short: such were the expressions of interest on the part of the neighborhood that Antonia decided to try something, and before the gathering broke she agreed to consult a legal expert to see what he counseled.

When Antonia returned from the consultation, paler than usual, women without their headscarves came out of every little run-down shop and ground floor to ask her questions, and exclamations of horror were heard. The law, instead of providing protection, compelled her to live conjugally under the same roof with the murderer!

"What laws, dear God above! The scoundrels who make them should have to abide by them!" the entire group cried out indignantly. "Isn't there any recourse, woman, any recourse at all?"

"He says we can separate . . . after something they call divorce."

"And what's divorce?"

"A very long lawsuit."

All the women dropped their arms in dismay: lawsuits never came to an end, and it was even worse if they did because the poor and innocent always lost.

"And to get one," the cleaning woman added, "I would first have to prove that my husband was mistreating me."

"Good Lord! Well, didn't that brute kill your mother? Wasn't that mistreatment? Huh? And doesn't the whole world know that he's threatened to kill you too?"

"But since nobody heard him say it . . . The lawyer says there has to be clear proof . . ."

A revolt of sorts broke out. There were women determined, they said, to present a petition to the very king himself, seeking a rescission of the pardon. And by turns they slept in the cleaning lady's house so that the poor woman could herself get some sleep. Fortunately, three days later news arrived that the pardon was partial, and that the convict still had a few more years to drag shackles around. The night that Antonia found out was the first one in which she didn't sit bolt upright in bed, her eyes popping, calling for help.

After this scare, more than a year went by and the cleaning lady, dedicated to her humble household employment, enjoyed peace once again. One day, the manservant of the house where she was working thought he was doing a favor for the ashen-faced woman, whose husband was in prison, by informing her that the queen was going to have a baby* and that there would surely be pardons.

The cleaning lady, who was scrubbing floors when she heard this news, dropped the mop and, letting down the skirt that she wore gathered around her waist, left with the gait of an automaton, as silent and lifeless as a statue. In response to messages sent to her by the houses where she worked she said that she was ill, although in fact she was only experiencing a general depression, an inability to raise her arms to do labor of any sort. The day the queen gave birth she counted the cannon shots of the salute, whose reports were ringing inside her head, and since someone pointed out to her that the royal offspring was female, she began to clutch at the hope that a male would have prompted more pardons. Besides, why should her husband be included in the pardons? He had already been pardoned once, and his crime was horrendous—killing the defenseless old woman who wasn't doing him any harm, all for a few miserable gold coins! In her mind she pictured the terrible scene again and again. Did the beast who struck that frightful blow deserve a pardon? Antonia remembered that the injured woman's lips were white, and it seemed as if she could see the congealed blood at the foot of the cot.

She locked herself in her house and spent the time sitting in a small chair next to the hearth. Bah! If he was going to kill her, it was better to let herself die.

Only her little boy's plaintive voice drew her out of her self-absorption.

"Mother, I'm hungry. Mother, what is that at the door? Who's coming?"

Finally, one beautiful sunny morning she shrugged her shoulders and, taking a pile of dirty clothes, began to walk toward the laundry. To the solicitous questions that were asked her, she gave slow, monosyllabic answers, and her eyes wandered aimlessly over the lather that splashed her face.

Who brought the unexpected news to the laundry as Antonia was gathering up her washed and wrung-out clothes and was going to leave? Did someone concoct the idea for charitable purposes or was it one of those mysterious rumors, of unknown origin, that on the eve of great events for nations, or individuals, flutter and whisper in the air? The fact is that poor Antonia, on hearing it, instinctively placed her hand on her heart and fell backwards on the damp stones of the laundry.

"But, did he really die?" the early risers were asking those who had just arrived.

"Yes."

"I heard it at the market."

"And I heard it at the shop."

"Who told you?"

"Me? My husband."

"And who told your husband?"

"The captain's orderly."

"And who told the orderly?"

"His boss."

At this point the source seemed sufficiently authoritative; no one attempted to learn more and just accepted the news as reliable and valid. The criminal was dead, on the eve of the pardon, before serving a full sentence! Antonia the cleaning lady raised her head, and for the first time her cheeks were tinged with a healthy color, and she burst into tears. She was weeping for joy and none of the onlookers was shocked. She was the pardoned one—her happiness was a just one. The tears bunched together at the corners of her eyes, swelling her heart, because ever since the crime she had dried up, that is, was unable to cry. Now she breathed deeply, free of the nightmare. The hand of Providence was so instrumental in what happened that it didn't occur to the cleaning lady that the news could be false.

That night, Antonia went to bed later than usual because she picked up her son at kindergarten and bought him some doughnuts, along with other sweets that the boy had wanted for some time. The two of them walked the streets, pausing in front of shop windows, with no desire to eat, thinking only about drinking in air, living life, and taking possession of it again.

Such was Antonia's absentmindedness that she didn't even notice that the door of her ground-floor room stood ajar. Without letting go of the boy's hand, she entered the confined area that served as living room, dining room, and kitchen, and stepped back, startled at seeing the oil lamp lit. A huge, black shape got up from the table, and the scream that was rising to the cleaning lady's lips was stifled in her throat.

It was he. Antonia, motionless, glued to the floor, couldn't actually see him yet, although his sinister image was mirrored in her wide-open eyes. Her rigid body underwent a momentary paralysis. Her cold hands let go of the boy, who, terrified, clutched at his mother's skirt. The husband spoke:

"You didn't expect me now, did you?" he murmured in a husky but calm tone.

At the sound of that voice, in which Antonia believed she could still hear the echoes of his curses and death threats, the miserable woman, as if awakening from a nightmare, uttered a piercing "Oh!" and, gathering up her son in her arms, broke out in a run toward the door. He cut her off.

"Hey, hey! Where are you going, lady of the house?" he stressed the words syllable by syllable with his convict's irony. "To stir up the neighborhood, now, at this hour? Everybody here keep still."

The last words were spoken without any accompanying aggressive gesture, but in a tone that curdled Antonia's blood. Nevertheless, her initial shock changed into feverish excitement—the lucid feverish excitement born of the instinct of self-preservation. A sudden thought flashed through her mind: seek protection through the child. His father had never seen him, but after all, he was his father! She held him up, near the light.

"Is this the kid?" the convict murmured, taking the oil lamp down from the wall and holding it close to the child's face.

The boy, blinded, was blinking his eyes and placing his hands in front of his face, as if to defend himself against that unknown father whose name he heard pronounced with terror and universal condemnation. He hugged his mother, who nervously hugged him back, her face whiter than a sheet.

"What an ugly runt!" grunted the father, hanging up the oil lamp again. "He looks as if the witches sucked him dry."

Antonia, without letting go of the boy, leaned against the wall because she was becoming faint. The room was spinning around her and she saw little blue flashes in the air.

"Look, isn't there anything to eat in this house?" her husband demanded.

Antonia sat the boy in a corner, on the floor, and while he cried from fear, stifling his sobs, his mother began to scurry about the room and set the table with trembling hands. She took out bread, a bottle of wine, removed from the hearth a codfish casserole and took great pains to serve him quickly, to placate her enemy with her zeal. The convict sat down and began to eat voraciously, taking frequent drinks of wine. She remained standing, eyeing with fascination that dry, clean-shaven, leathery face that shone with an unmistakable prison sheen. He filled his glass again and invited her to join him.

"I don't want any," Antonia stammered. The wine, in the reflection of the oil lamp, looked to her like a blood clot.

He polished it off with a shrug of the shoulders and ladled himself more cod, which he devoured greedily, using his fingers and chewing huge chunks of bread. His wife watched him as he gorged himself, and a tenuous hope began to work its way into her spirit: that when he finished eating, he'd leave without killing her. Afterwards, she would lock the door securely, and then if he wanted to kill her the neighborhood would be awake and would hear her screams. Just that it would probably be impossible for her to scream! She cleared her throat to steady her voice. Her husband, who had just barely finished stuffing himself, pulled out a cigar tucked inside a waist pocket, clipped it with his fingernail and calmly lit it in the oil lamp.

"Hey . . . Where are you going?" he shouted, seeing that his wife was inching furtively toward the door. "None of that."

"To put the little one to bed," she answered without realizing what she was saying.

Antonia took refuge in the adjoining room, carrying her son in her arms. Surely the murderer wouldn't enter there. How would he have the nerve to do such a thing? It was the room in which he had committed the crime, her mother's bedroom. Before the murder, the married couple used to sleep next door, but the destitution that ensued after the old woman's death forced Antonia to sell the double bed and use her deceased mother's. Thinking she was out of danger, she began to undress the child, who now dared to cry more openly, his face buried in her bosom, but the door opened and the convict walked in.

Antonia watched him cast a sidelong glance all around the

room; and he very cooly took off his shoes, removed his belt, and, finally, lay down on the victim's bed. The cleaning lady thought she was dreaming. If her husband opened a knife, he would probably frighten her less than with his display of such a horrible calm. He stretched and turned over on the sheets, finishing off his cigar stub and sighing contently, like a tired man who finds a soft, clean bed.

"And you?" he said, talking to Antonia. "What are you doing there, frozen like a statue? Aren't you coming to bed?"

"I'm . . . not sleepy," she stammered, her teeth chattering.

"So what if you're not sleepy? Are you going to spend the night on guard duty?"

"There . . . there . . . isn't room . . . for both of us. You sleep. I'll stay here, I can make do . . ."

He swore several times.

"Are you afraid of me? Do I disgust you? What the hell is going on here? You'd better come to bed, because if you don't . . ."

Her husband sat up and extended his hands, showing that he intended to jump out of bed. But Antonia, with the fatalistic submission of a slave, was already beginning to undress. Her hurrying fingers tore at ribbons, violently pulled out hooks and eyes, and ripped up petticoats. In a corner of the room were heard the stifled sobs of the little boy.

And it was the little boy who, screaming frantically, at dawn called the neighbor women who found Antonia in bed, stretched out as if dead. The doctor came quickly and declared that she was alive; he attempted to bleed her, but couldn't draw out a single drop of blood. She passed away twenty-four hours later, of a natural death, because she bore no lesions whatsoever. The little boy assured them that the man who had spent the night there called her repeatedly on getting up, and seeing that she wasn't responding, ran off like a madman.

A Descendant of the Cid*

The elderly priest of the shrine of San Clemente de Boán was seated at the table, eating supper peacefully in a corner of his spacious kitchen. The light from the triple-burner oil lamp highlighted the prominent lines of his face and thick, gray eyebrows. Shocks of white hair still covered his tonsured head while ruddy, blood-red skin spilled out in sturdy folds from his clerical collar.

The priest sat at the head of the table; at the center, his nephew, a good-looking youth twenty-two years old, was putting away his portion with gusto; and at the far end, the farm hand, the sleeves of his coarse linen shirt rolled up to his elbows, was dipping a wooden spoon into an enormous bowl of steaming broth and quietly transferring it to his stomach.

They were being served by a village girl who took advantage of the opportunity to have her finger in the pie too, if not in the actual plate, in the conversation.

Her undemanding table duties allowed her to join in because they consisted of nothing more than placing before the diners a gigantic chunk of bread, taking wine and earthenware dishes from the cupboard, and carelessly pushing across the tablecloth the huge clay casserole that was overflowing with greasy potatoes.

"Master Javier," she asked during one of these operations, "what have you heard about the band of robbers* who are in the area?"

"About the robbers, girl? Wait a minute . . . ," replied the youth, as he raised his dark, animated face. "What have I heard about the robbers? Well . . . I was told something at the fair . . . Yes, I was told . . ."

"It's said that Fr. Lubrego was robbed of a huge amount of money . . . something like one hundred *onzas*. They waited until he went to the fair of the fifteenth* to sell his oxen and the rye that he stored in the granary, and then they jumped him."

30

"Didn't he put up a fight?"

"Don't you know that he's getting on in years? And to make matters worse, around the time of the robbery he was laid up in bed with gout."

The priest, who until then had kept quiet, suddenly raised his eyes, which underneath his snow-white eyebrows shone like jet beads, and exclaimed:

"What do you mean put up a fight! Never in his life has Lubrego learned how to hold a shotgun."

"He's old."

"Bah! As far as being old . . . I'll be sixty-five on Pentecost, and he'll be sixty-six on Corpus Christi. I have it on good authority. He himself told me. So age . . . As for me, it hasn't affected my aim."

His nephew agreed enthusiastically. "For sure. The partridges that we bagged yesterday can testify to it, right? You got the last one for me."

"And the hare today, eh, my boy?"

"And the fox on Sunday," interposed the farm hand, turning his face away from the steaming broth. "When the Reverend Father dragged him here on a rope like this (and he squeezed his throat) he was yelping furiously. Ooo . . . ooo . . ."

"There's the cursed creature," the priest mumbled, pointing toward the door where a bloody hide was spread and nailed at the four points.

"You won't eat any more chickens," the servant girl added, threatening the remains of the animal with her fist.

This conversation about hunting restored the group's peace of mind and Javier gave no further thought to telling what he knew about the band of robbers. The priest, after giving thanks by muttering some Latin, rinsed his mouth with wine, crossed his legs, lit a cigarette, and, handing the folded newspaper to his nephew, mumbled between puffs:

"Well, my boy, let's see what's in *La Fe*."

Javier began to read an editorial, and the servant girl, without thinking about clearing the table, took a cup of broth for herself from the pot and sat down to have it on a bench next to the hearth. All of a sudden a loud, prolonged howl drowned out the reader's voice. The servant girl froze with her spoon held in the air, not taking it to her mouth; Javier listened attentively for a second, and then resumed reading; while the priest, indifferent to the noise, exhaled puffs of smoke and spat frequently out of the side of his mouth. Two minutes went by, and another howl, followed by furious barking, broke the silence outside. This time the reader dropped his newspaper and the servant girl rose, stammering:

"Master Javier . . . My lord . . . My lord . . ."

"Quiet," Javier commanded, and on tiptoe he approached the window where the dogs' racket seemed to rise from below. But suddenly the noise abated.

The priest, cupping his ear with his right hand, was paying close attention from his seat.

"Uncle," Javier whispered.

"Yes?"

"The dogs have quieted down but I'd swear I hear voices."

"Then how did they quiet down?"

The youth did not reply—he was busy removing the crossbar from the window with as little noise as possible. Gently he half-opened the shutters, raised the bolt, and, encouraged by the silence, determined to push open the glass window. A piercing cold swept into the room; there was a glimpse of black sky studded with stars, and silhouetted in the distance were the vague contours of the forest trees, gloomy and bunched together. At almost the same moment a sharp whistle rent the air, a shot was heard, and a bullet, grazing the top of Javier's hair, slammed into the opposite wall. He instinctively closed the window, and the priest, rushing to his nephew's side, began to feel him anxiously.

"Why . . . the scoundrels! Did it hit you, boy?"

"Good thing they're not using buckshot or I'd be in fine shape," Javier remarked, somewhat shaken.

"Are they out there?"

"Behind the first row of chestnut trees in the grove."

"Engage the bolt . . . that's it. Now, on the double, get the shotgun, the cartridges, the powder flask. Bring the *Lafuché** too. Do you hear?"

At this point the priest had to raise his voice as if he were commanding a military operation because the dogs' desperate barking was getting louder and louder.

"Now they're barking out there. Confounded animals, why do you suppose they were quiet before?"

"They must have recognized one of the robbers, who probably whistled to them or talked to them," suggested the farm hand, who was on his feet clutching a pitchfork used for gathering gorse, while the servant girl, huddled near the fire, was trembling all over and uttering a mousy squeal every now and then.

The priest, opening a peephole cut into the shutters of the window, put his fist through it and broke the glass. He immediately pressed his mouth to the opening and in a powerful voice shouted to the dogs:

"Chucho, Morito, Linda, sic 'em! Chucho, rip 'em apart! Come on, Linda, tear 'em to pieces!"

The barking changed from rabid to frenzied. At the foot of the very same window sounds of a struggle were heard. Muffled threats followed, a screech of pain, a curse, and the whimper of a dying animal.

"Poor Morito . . . He won't chase any more foxes," the farm hand mumbled.

In the meantime, the priest, having taken his shotgun from Javier's hands, was loading it with uncommon dispatch.

"Me, I'm more comfortable with my trusty old partridge shotgun. You use the *Lafuché*. What do I know about these newfangled firearms? Bah, I'm for the old-fashioned Spanish model. Do you have cartridges?"

"Yes, sir," answered Javier, preparing to load the carbine too.

"Are they down there now?"

"At the very foot of the window. They may be putting the ladders in place."

"Any danger of them getting in through the main door?"

"I don't think so. They have to jump over the corral wall and we can shoot them from the veranda."

"And through the wine cellar door?"

"If they set fire to it . . . But break it down, they can't."

"Well, we're going to have some fun for a while. Sit back and wait, my friends, sit back and wait."

Javier looked at his uncle's face. His nostrils were flared, there was a sardonic twist to his lips, the tip of his tongue was showing between his teeth, his cheeks were flushed, and his eyes were sparkling, the same as when his favorite setter stopped in the mountains to point to a flock of partridges hidden in the broom fields and flower-covered valleys.

For his part, Javier was horrified by those preparations for a human hunt. In moments of such critical consequence, while the shell slid into the breech, he was thinking that he would be much more comfortable in the cloisters of the university, at the café, or at the fair of the fifteenth, buying crullers and caramels for the young ladies of the Valdomar manor. He imagined the fair again: the oxen's shiny flanks, the cows' gentle air, the hacks' shabby coats. And he heard the clear voice of Casildita del Pazo, who was saying to him in the drawn out, mellifluous accent of the area:

"Oh, give me your arm, for goodness sake or I won't be able to move with all these people!"

He thought he felt the pressure of a light arm. But no. It was the hairy, muscular hand of the priest who was motioning him toward the window.

"Let's put out the oil lamp," and he did so in three mighty puffs. "Let's begin the fun and games. I'll load, you shoot . . . then you load and I'll shoot. Hey, Tomasa!" he shouted to the servant girl. "Stop shrieking. You sound like the weasel . . . Start boiling water, oil, wine—as much as there is . . . You," he added, turning to the farm hand, "to the veranda. If they climb over the wall, you let me know."

He stopped talking and cautiously half-opened the window, leaving just a crack to accommodate the barrel of a shotgun and the watchful eye of a man. Javier shuddered when he felt the freezing night air, but he quickly recovered—for there was no cowardice in him—and looked below. A group of dark figures was congregating, and mysterious voices were heard, as if in consultation.

"Fire!" said his uncle in his ear.

"There are twenty or more," Javier retorted.

"So what!" the priest growled while pushing his nephew away with an impatient gesture. And supporting the barrel of the shotgun on the window sill, he fired.

There was a commotion in the group and the priest rubbed his hands with satisfaction.

"One of them was knocked right off his feet! *Quoniam!*" He mumbled the Latin word with which, ever since his seminary days, he replaced all the interjections that abound in the Spanish language. "Now it's your turn, boy. They have a ladder. The first one to climb it . . ."

Javier's fingers were twitching on his magnificent Lefaucheux carbine, but all at once they slackened.

"Uncle," he ventured to say in a hushed voice, "there are people down there that we know. I remember now what they were saying at the fair. They're certain that in the band are the surgeon from Solás, the fireworks maker from Gunsende, and the brother of the doctor from Doas. Do you want me to talk to them? With a little money maybe they'll be satisfied and leave us alone—nobody'll have to be killed."

"Money, money!" the priest exclaimed hoarsely. "You think undoubtedly that we've got millions here?"

"And the shrine's funds?"

"Belong to the shrine, *quoniam!* And first I'll let them roast my feet, as they did to the priest in Solás last year, than give them a cent. But it'd be much better to be cut to pieces all at once than be roasted alive. Shoot them! If you're afraid, I'll do it."

"Afraid, no," Javier declared, and he propped his carbine on the sill.

"Let them have both barrels," his uncle ordered.

Twice Javier squeezed the trigger, and from below the two blasts were greeted with a formidable clamor. The youth had not had time to withdraw his hand when a volley of shots smashed into the window panes ripping out splinters and shattering them into bits and pieces. The terrible din resulted from different reports: the sharp clap of pistol shots, the loud rumble of carbines, and the boom of blunderbusses and short rifles. Javier moved back, tottering, his right hand drooping; the carbine fell to the floor.

"What's the matter, boy?"

"They must've broken my wrist," groaned Javier, almost fainting and going to the bench to sit down.

The priest, who was loading his shotgun, then felt himself seized by the tails of his frock coat, and in the indistinct light of the fireplace he saw a wan apparition crawling at his feet. It was the servant girl, who was pronouncing words in a barely intelligible voice.

"Master . . . , master . . . , give up, master . . . , for the love of God . . . Master, they're going to kill us . . . all of us will die here . . ."

"Let go of me, *quoniam!*" the priest denounced her, dashing to the window.

Javier, disabled, was moaning as he tried to tie a handkerchief with his left hand. Paralyzed from terror, the servant girl did not get up, but the priest, paying no attention to the two invalids, quickly opened the shutters and saw a ladder leaning against the wall; he almost bumped into the heads of the two men who were scaling it. He fired at point-blank range and the one at the bottom fell off. Then he raised his shotgun, brandished it by the barrel, and with one blow of the butt drove the one at the top tumbling to the ground. Several shots were fired at him, but the priest had already withdrawn, and was inside reloading his weapon.

Javier, who was no longer groaning, approached him resolutely.

"At this rate, Uncle, you won't hold out even for a quarter of an hour. They're going to get in through there or through the patio. I've picked up the smell of oil; they'll probably set fire to the wine cellar door. I can't shoot and I'd like to do something to help you."

"Pour boiling oil on them with your left hand."

"I'm going to take Rabona out of the stable through the main gate and ride as fast as I can to Doas."

"To the Civil Guard barracks?"

"To the Civil Guard barracks."

"There's not enough time now. I'll be dead. Goodbye, my boy. Say an Our Father for me and have some Masses said.

"Come on wad, get in there!"

"Pretend that you're surrendering! Keep them busy. I'll go like a blue streak!"

For an instant the youth's black silhouette screened the red reflection on the fireplace wall, and then he disappeared in the darkness of the veranda. His uncle shrugged and, leaning out the window, again fired his shotgun blindly. He then ran to the fireplace where he vigorously unhooked the heavy pot, hung from a long iron chain, that was boiling over the live coals. He opened the window completely, no longer taking precautions, raised the pot and dumped its contents all at once on top of his enemies. A tremendous, agonizing howl was heard, and as if the burning liquid had ignited the rage excited in them by that heroic defense, they all threw themselves at the ladder, some climbing over the shoulders of others; and while two or three of them were slipping down the mud walls and exchanging blows with the farm hand, a human wave fell on the priest, who was still fighting back swinging the butt of his shotgun. When the cluster of men split up, the old man could be seen, spread out on the floor with his hands tied, by the light of the oil lamp that had been lit.

The bandits' soot-blackened faces, false beards, handkerchiefs tied around their necks, wide-brimmed hats, and other trappings lent them a diabolical appearance. Their leader was a tall, resolute, and laconic man who in seconds ordered the door closed and the farm hand and servant girl bound and gagged. One of his men said something to him in a low voice, and afterwards he approached the vanquished priest.

"Hey, Reverend Father. Don't play dead. There's a man out there that you wounded and he wants to make his confession."

They were awkwardly climbing the interior stairs of the wine cellar, transporting something. They came into view when they reached the kitchen; it was four men carrying another, held high, who was trailing pools of blood. The wounded bandit's head was swinging gently. His eyes, which were becoming glazed, looked like porcelain beads set in his blackened face, and his mouth hung half-open.

"What do you mean, confession!" the leader said. "He's at death's door!"

But they had no sooner set him on the bench, supporting his head, when the dying man moved, and his expression revived.

"Confession!" he exclaimed in a loud, clear voice.

They untied the priest and shoved him to the foot of the bench. The wounded man's lips were moving as if he were reciting the act of contrition. The priest recognized the death rattle and noticed pink foam forming at the corners of the robber's mouth. He raised his hand and pronounced *Ego te absolvo* at the instant that the man's head was falling on his chest for the last time.

"Take him away from here," the leader ordered. "Now, priest, tell us where your money's hidden."

"I have nothing to give you," he responded firmly.

The priest's eyebrows were knitted, and his skin, no longer ruddy, exhibited the jaundiced pallor of rage; his hands, bruised and strangulated by the cord, trembled with the violent shaking of old age.

"You'll change your tune in about ten minutes. We're going to fry your fingers in some of the same oil that you threw at us. We're going to seat you on hot coals. One . . . two . . ."

The priest looked around, and on the table where they had eaten supper he saw the knife used for cutting bread. He flung himself with the quickness of a cat to seize it, knocking over the table and oil lamp with one kick; and then, barricaded behind the table, he began to defend himself blindly, in the dark, without feeling the blows that struck him—thinking only of dying nobly while he was being riddled with bullets at point-blank range.

The sergeant from the Civil Guard at Doas, who arrived at the scene of the struggle a half hour later, while the highwaymen were still searching futilely for the priest's money under the rafters, among the cornhusks stuffed into his mattress, and even in his breviary, assured me that the body did not have human form —it was that full of holes, battered, and bruised. The same sergeant also told me that since the death of the priest of Boán partridges are plentiful; and at the fair he pointed out Javier to me—he doesn't hunt any wild game now because his right hand is maimed.

First Prize

Back in the time of Godoy,* the fortune of the Torres-Nobles family of Fuencar figured among the most secure and powerful in the Spanish monarchy. Political vicissitudes and other setbacks depleted income little by little, and in the end it was squandered completely by the last Marquis of Torres-Nobles, a spendthrift rake who caused a lot of talk in the court when Narváez* was a young man.

When he was almost sixty, the Marquis of Torres-Nobles made the decision to retire to his country estate in Fuencar, the only one of his properties not mortgaged. There he devoted himself completely to attending to his health, in no less a state of ruin than the family wealth; and since Fuencar still brought in enough for him to live in relative comfort, he organized his household so that he was not wanting for any conveniences. He engaged a chaplain who, in addition to saying Mass for him on Sundays and holy days of obligation, was his partner in bezique and other card games (such simple pastimes amused the ex-seducer greatly) and read to him and commented on the most reactionary political newspapers; a majordomo or overseer who collected cash on the barrelhead when it was due and ably directed the farm chores; an obese, phlegmatic coachman who handled with a grave air the reins of the two mules who pulled the calash; a quiet, solicitous housekeeper, not so young that she was a temptation nor so old that she was repulsive; a valet brought from Madrid, a carryover and relic of the dissolute life of the past, turning over a new leaf like his master, as discreet and reliable now as he was then; and lastly, a cook as clean as can be, with exquisite hands for preparing all the dishes of that classic national cuisine that satisfied the stomach without irritating it and delighted the palate without corrupting it. With such excellent domestic help, the marquis's house ran like a well-regulated clock, and the master rejoiced more and more in having left the gulf of Madrid to come into port and lay to for repairs. His health was being restored; sleep, digestion, and other functions necessary to the well-being of this scant, perishable tunic that incarcerates the spirit were being regularized, and in not too many months the Marquis of Torres-Nobles put on weight without losing agility, straightened his posture somewhat, and his fresh breath indicated that a fierce gastralgia no longer gnawed at his stomach.

If the marquis lived well, his servants didn't live too badly either. To keep them from leaving him, he paid higher wages than anyone else in the province, and moreover, from time to time he would treat and pamper them with gifts. Thus were they kept happy: not too much work, which was methodical and invariable, and generous pay occasionally augmented by little surprises from the openhanded marquis.

In the month of December the year before last it was colder than usual, and the pastureland and surrounding area of Fuencar were buried under a layer of snow about eight and a half inches high. One night, fleeing the solitude of his huge study, the marquis went down to the kitchen of the farmhouse in search of his staff because he craved human company; he huddled near the fireplace, warmed the palms of his hands by snapping his fingers, and he even laughed at the stories told with Andalusian wit by the overseer and shepherd, and observed that the cook had very pretty eyes. Among the conversations of a more or less peasant nature that amused him, he heard that all of his servants planned to pool their resources to buy a tenth part of a Christmas lottery ticket.

Very early the following day the marquis dispatched a messenger to the neighboring city; it was getting dark when the benign master entered the kitchen waving a few pieces of paper and announcing to his servants, with genuine warmth, that he had fulfilled their wishes by obtaining a lottery ticket for the next drawing, and that he was giving them as a gift two tenth parts, keeping eight for himself to try his luck too. When the servants heard the news, there was an explosion of joy in the kitchen, with *vivas* and exaggerated blessings invoked; only the shepherd, a white-haired, sarcastic, and sententious old man, shook his head, affirming that whoever cast his lot with masters "scared

luck away," which the marquis deplored so much he decreed
that the shepherd not share at all in the two tenth parts.

That night the marquis didn't sleep as soundly as he usually
did since Fuencar had become his refuge; a few concerns of the
kind that only torment confirmed bachelors kept him awake. He
hadn't liked at all the eagerness with which his servants spoke
about the money that could come their way. "These people," the
marquis was saying to himself, "would only wait to fill their
pockets to leave me high and dry. And what plans they have!
Celedonio (the coachman) talked of going into the tavern business . . . doubtless to drink up the wine! Then that simpleton
Doña Rita (the housekeeper) dreams of establishing a boardinghouse! I must say, as for Jacinto (the valet), he certainly kept
things to himself, but he was looking out of the corner of his eye
at Pepa (the cook) who, well, has her charm . . . I'd swear they
plan to get married. Bah (on exclaiming *bah*, the Marquis of
Torres-Nobles turned over in bed and wrapped himself up because he felt the cold going down the back of his neck)! In a
nutshell, what does all of it matter to me? We're not going to win
first prize, so . . . they'll have to wait for whatever bequests I leave
them." A short time later the kindly old man was snoring.

Two days later the drawing was to take place, and Jacinto, who
was as clever as they come, arranged things in such a way that his
master had to send him to the city in search of certain supplies or
indispensable items. Night was falling, it was snowing heavily,
and Jacinto still had not returned, despite having left very early
in the morning. As usual, the servants were gathered in the
kitchen when they heard the dull sound of the horse's hooves
on the fresh snow, and a man in whom they recognized their
companion Jacinto, burst upon them like a bombshell. He was
pale and shaking and greatly agitated, and in a choked voice
exclaimed:

"First prize!"

At the time the marquis was in his study, his legs wrapped in
a close-woven blanket and puffing on a cigar, while the chaplain
read him the petty politics of *El Siglo Futuro*. Abruptly inter-
rupting the reading, both lent an ear to the racket that came from
the kitchen. At first it seemed to them that the servants were
arguing, but after several seconds of paying close attention they

became convinced that the shouting was in fact jubilation, although so discordant and delirious that the marquis, vexed and considering his dignity compromised, sent the chaplain to learn what was going on and to impose silence. The envoy returned in less than three minutes and, collapsing on the divan, said out of breath: "I'm suffocating." And he peeled off his clerical collar and tore his vest while attempting to unbutton it. The marquis rushed to his aid, and fanning his face with *El Siglo Futuro* managed to hear him blurt out in faltering speech:

"We've w . . . w. . . won first prize . . . first . . ."

In spite of his infirmities, the marquis bounded to the kitchen with unheard-of quickness and stopped at the threshold, amazed by the strange scene that was taking place there. Celedonio and Doña Rita were dancing—I don't know if it was the *jaleo* or the *cachucha**—and slapping their shoes in mid-air, jumping up and down like sinuous, electrified rag dolls; Jacinto, holding onto a chair for a dance partner, was waltzing swiftly and amorously; Pepa was banging a frying pan with the handle of a ladle, making unpleasant music; and the overseer, stretched out on the floor, was turning over and over, shouting, or rather, howling wildly, "Long live the Virgin!" As soon as they caught sight of the marquis, the servants gone-mad threw themselves at him with open arms, and since he lacked the strength to avoid it, they lifted him in the air; singing and dancing and tossing him from one to another like a rubber ball, they paraded him all around the kitchen until they saw that he was furious and set him down. What happened next was even worse; Pepa, the cook, seized his waist, and whether he wanted to or not, dragged him through a dizzy *galop* while the overseer, handing him a wineskin, insisted that he try a swig, assuring him that the spirits were exquisite, something that he knew for a fact after having imbibed almost all the red wine that it held.

As soon as the marquis was able to break loose, he took refuge in his room with the intention of venting his anger by recounting to the chaplain his servants' boldness and chatting with him about the first prize. Much to his surprise he saw that the chaplain, wrapped in his long cloak and pulling his hat down, was getting ready to leave.

"Don Calixto, my good man, where are you going?" exclaimed the marquis in astonishment.

Well, with his approval, Don Calixto was going to Seville, to see his family, to tell them the good news, to collect in person his tenth-part share, a sweet sum that amounted to thousands of duros.*

"And you're leaving me now? And Mass? And . . . ?"

Just then the valet stuck his pointed nose in the doorway. If the marquis gave him permission, he too would depart to collect what was coming to him. The marquis raised his voice, saying that they had to be out of their minds to set out at such an hour and in eight and a half inches of snow, to which Don Calixto and Jacinto responded of one mind that the train stopped at the next station at twelve o'clock, which they would reach on foot or however they could. The marquis was just opening his mouth to say, "Jacinto will stay because I need him," when in turn the ruddy face of the coachman appeared, framed by the doorway; without asking the marquis's consent and with insolent pleasure, he was coming to say goodbye to his master because he was quitting—so there!—to pick up all that "dough."

"And the mules?" the master shouted. "And the carriage, who will drive it, I want to know?"

"Whomever Your Excellency orders . . . since I don't expect to drive a carriage any more," the coachman responded, turning his back and making way for Doña Rita, who came in not as usual—the timid housekeeper who entered carefully, but with a disheveled appearance, and somewhat boisterous and smiling, waving a heavy bunch of keys which she handed over to the marquis, pointing out to him:

"Your Excellency should know that this is the one to the pantry . . . this is to the clothes closet . . . this one is for . . ."

"The devil deal with you and your entire caste, diabolic witch! Now you want me to get out the salt pork and chickpeas, huh? You go to . . ."

Doña Rita didn't hear the end of the curse because she went out whistling; the others who had spoken with the marquis left after she did, and then, right behind them was the furious marquis himself. He followed them from room to room and was on the verge of catching up in the kitchen, but, to avoid braving the freezing weather, didn't dare continue pursuing them to the patio. By the light of the moon that gave a silvery color to the snow-covered ground, the marquis watched them go off: Don Calixto in front, then Celedonio and Doña Rita arm-in-arm, and, lastly, Jacinto sticking very close to the female silhouette that he recognized as being Pepa the cook. Pepilla too! The marquis glanced about the deserted kitchen, noticed that the fireplace fire was dying out, and heard an animal-like snore. At the foot of the chimney, with his legs spread wide apart, the overseer was sleeping off a hangover.

The following morning the shepherd who refused "to scare luck away," sautéed some leftovers of bread with a clove of garlic for the Marquis of Torres-Nobles, and thus was this noble gentleman able to eat a hot meal the first day that he awoke as a millionaire.

It seems superfluous to me to describe the marquis's sumptuous relocation in Madrid; what surely should not be omitted is that he hired a cook whose dishes were so many gastronomic poems. It's suspected that the delicacies prepared by such a sublime artist, savored with excessive relish by the marquis, caused the illness that took him to his grave. Nevertheless, I believe that the fright and fall that he suffered when his magnificent English horses bolted was the real cause of his passing, which occurred shortly after occupying the mansion that he furnished on Alcalá Street.

When the marquis's will was opened, it was learned that he named the shepherd of Fuencar his heir.

On the Streetcar

The last cold waves of winter give way to the spring season, and some life-giving current drifts in the atmosphere and rises to the firmament's unadulterated blueness. People returning from Mass or their morning dash through the streets storm the Salamanca district streetcar at the Puerta del Sol. The women wear simple morning clothes; the shadowy outlines of the silk lace of their mantillas frame the glow of black eyes; wound around their wrists are rosaries; and in their gloved hands they conceal the handles of parasols and carry bunches of lilacs or paper cones full of sweets that dangle by narrow ribbons from their little fingers. Some are accompanied by their children, and what well-dressed, well-groomed and nice-looking children they are! You feel like smothering them with kisses; there's an irresistible impulse to run your fingers through the thick, wavy blonde hair that reaches their shoulders.

Very nearby, almost opposite me, a baby just a few months old stands out. The only thing you can see of him, aside from his chubby little face and pink hands, are pieces of lace, strips of cloth embroidered with eyelets, ribbon bows, all of it white, and two balls wrapped in wool which is also white—the restless, dancing balls that are his tiny feet. He raises himself on them, bounces happily, and when a fortyish gentleman next to him, probably his father, makes a funny face at him or strikes a match for him, the infant laughs heartily with his drooling, toothless mouth reminiscent of an old man's and radiates light from heaven in his innocent eyes. Further away, a little girl of about nine lounges in a disdainful, listless posture, showing off one of her slender, crossed legs covered with taut, black silk stockings, and swinging a foot inside a patent leather English shoe. The future beauty already displays signs of coquetry; she knows that people look at and admire her, and she lets herself be looked at and admired with a hidden, inner satisfaction, making a face

45

equivalent to saying, 'I know you find me attractive; I know you're watching me.' Her faintly wavy, neat, smooth, luxuriant, and magnificent head of hair envelops and surrounds her with a golden halo, hovering under the wide felt hat obscured by an enormous gray feather. Pressed against her chest she holds a package wrapped in silky paper, most likely a well-made toy for her younger brother, maybe a surprise for her mama, a bow or a topknot that her precocious presumption impelled her to buy. Beyond this closed flower bud sits another that is blossoming, her sister perhaps, a lovely creature of maybe twenty, a refined example of the Madrilenian brunette, simply dressed and wearing an almost invisible small bonnet that heightens her delicate, serious profile. Not far from her a haughty matron with freshly applied rice powder on her face lowers her eyes and concentrates hard as if to dream or remember.

Carrying such passengers, the plebeian streetcar sparkles proudly in the sun, no more nor less than if it were a landau upholstered in satin, pulled by a team of genuine English horses. Its windows look clear; its metal knobs dazzle; its mules trot along spiritedly and gracefully; the conductor urges them on in a lively voice; and the collector, attentive and solicitous, asks for the tickets and presents the white or rose stubs with a courteous gesture. Instead of the foul odor usually given off by the carloads of workers over on the Pacífico and Hipódromo lines, flowery aromas, a sanitary whiff, and the fresh smell of laundered linen pervade the atmosphere of the streetcar. If a coin falls to the floor when payment is being made, the passenger who looks for it catches a glimpse of tiny feet, Louis XV–style high heels, petticoat ruffles, and petite ankles. As the car moves up along Alcalá Street, the sun shines brighter and a greater sense of *joie de vivre* is produced by the Sunday bustle, the throngs that swarm on the sidewalks, the rapid crisscrossing of coaches, the light of day, and the mild temperature. Oh, how gay the Madrilenian Sunday is and how aristocratic the streetcar at that time of day when throughout all the houses of the area one hears the clatter of dishes—the herald of lunch—and crystal fruit bowls only await the choice fruit or tempting candy selected in person by the mistress of the house at Martinho's shop or Prast's!

I noticed but one blemish in the makeup of the streetcar. It's true that this blot was black as can be and as ugly as sin, although perhaps it just seemed that way by virtue of the contrast. A lower-class woman huddled in a corner, caressing the child in her arms. It was impossible to determine her age; she could just as easily have been in her thirties as in her forties. She was as thin as a rail and her drab shawl, on its last legs, highlighted the meagerness of her limbs—it looked as if it were hung on a coat rack. The shawl of Madrid's lower-class women has its own character, an eloquent, telling one; if there is no other article of clothing that better enhances the graceful curves, that better accentuates the provocative hip swinging in impulsive, common Madrilenian women, neither is there one that reveals more the abject poverty, the wearying discouragement of a wretched, miserable life, the emaciation of hunger, the supreme indifference to pain, the absolute lack of pretentions in those women whom adversity has battered, and who have completely renounced not only the expectation of pleasing, but also the prestige of their sex.

I suspected that the woman in the ash-colored shawl, indigent beyond the shadow of a doubt, suffered from a grief even more cruel than penury. Penury by itself is accepted with cheerful resignation by Spaniards, who up to a short time ago were oblivious of socialist demands. Poverty is the fate of the poor and protesting is futile. What I saw stamped on that face more livid than pallid, on that mouth sunken at the corners where it seemed that laughter had never frolicked, in those burned-out eyes with inflamed, bloodshot eyelids and bereft of soothing tears, was something more terrible, more exceptional than penury: it was despair.

The little boy slept. Compared with the woman's outfit, the child's was brand-new and decent. His woolen socks showed no big tears; his rough but strong shoes were in good condition; his coarse jacket undoubtedly kept him warm; and what could be seen of his face, a little cheek flushed from sleep, looked clean and clear. A red beret covered his bald head. He slept peacefully; you couldn't even tell that he was breathing. From time to time, the woman, as if instinctively, would hug the boy, fondling him gently with her trembling, blackish, scrawny hand.

The collector approached her with his small receipt book, jingling the change in his moneybag. The woman shuddered as if she were awakening from a dream; she searched her pocketbook and brought out, after exploring for a long time, a copper coin.

"Where to?"

"To the end of the line."

"It's fifteen *centimes* from the Puerta del Sol, madam," he pointed out, midway between irritable and sympathetic, "and here you're giving me ten."

"Ten!" the woman repeated vaguely, as if she were thinking about something. "Ten."

"Yes, ten. A ten-*centime* piece. Don't you see it?"

"Well, I don't have any more," the woman responded softly and indifferently.

"Well, the fare is fifteen," the collector reminded her with a touch of sternness in his voice, unable to grumble too much because pity prevented him.

Meanwhile, people on the streetcar were beginning to find out about the incident, and one lady was already looking in her change purse to make up the insignificant shortfall.

"I don't have any more," the woman repeated obstinately, without getting angry or distressed. Even before the lady handed over the five-*centime* piece, the collector turned around and shrugged his shoulders, like someone who says: 'This kind of thing happens every now and then.' Suddenly, when it was least expected, the woman, still cradling her son, sat up, and with her eyes blazing, exclaimed furiously to those present:

"My husband left me for another woman!"

One person frowned, another suppressed laughter. At first we thought that the miserable woman had gone mad to shout like that at the top of her lungs and blurt out such an incongruity, but she didn't even notice the onlookers' astonished reaction.

"He left me for another woman," she repeated in the midst of silence and general curiosity. "A hussy all made-up and painted like a wall. He took off with her. He gives her everything he makes, and me he beat. Me he clubbed on the head. It's all bruised. The worst thing is that he's gone. I don't know where he is. And for two months I haven't known."

After saying this, she collapsed in her corner, absent-mindedly adjusting the cotton headscarf that she wore tied under her chin.

She trembled as if her insides were churning, and two hot little tears streamed from her bloodshot eyes and rolled down her emaciated cheeks. She muttered incoherently the rest of her lament, the cruel details of the domestic drama. I heard the fortyish gentleman, who was striking matches to entertain the tot, murmur in the ear of the lady next to him:

"That poor devil . . . I can understand her husband. She looks like an old rag. And that puss and those beady eyes!"

The very same lady tugged lightly at the collector's sleeve and handed him something. The collector approached the woman and placed the alms in her hand.

"Here. That lady is giving you a *peseta*."

There occurred instantaneously a contagious outpouring. Every passenger in the streetcar was overcome by a desire to contribute. Pocketbooks, wallets, and purses were brought out. The collection was as sudden as it was relatively generous.

Whether because the woman's desperate tone had softened and stirred all their hearts, or whether because it is easier to be willing to throw in the first *peseta* rather than the last five, everybody tried to give at once. Even the disdainful little girl with the big mop of blond hair, perhaps understanding in the midst of her innocence that great distress was to be consoled there, made the most adorably sincere and winsome facial expression and said to her older sister: "María, something for the poor woman." The strange thing was that the latter showed neither contentment nor gratitude for the manna that fell on her. Evidently her grief figured on the list of those that weren't alleviated by the sprinkling of money. She kept, of course, what the collector handed over to her, and with a nod indicated that she was acknowledging the charity—nothing more. It wasn't disdain, it wasn't pride, it wasn't a moral inability to recognize the good deed: it was absorption in a greater distress, in a fixed idea that the woman followed through space with a visionary gaze, her body in an epileptic shake.

Even so, her attitude brought about immediate relief from the sympathetic reaction. The person who gives alms is almost always a leading egoist who longs for the wave of the magic wand that transforms tears into joy. Utter desperation disorients him, and as a declaration of independence proclaimed by the poor, even manages to damage his self-respect. It could be said that the people on the streetcar were a bit embarrassed at their compassionate outburst when they noticed that after the shower of single and multiple *pesetas*, including a brand-new, shiny five-*peseta* coin, from the baby boy, the woman didn't liven up at all, nor did she pay them any attention whatsoever. Naturally this is not the kind of thought that is stated out loud, and as a result nobody said it to anybody; they all kept it to themselves and feigned indifference, affecting a seemly distraction and talking about things in no way related to what had taken place. "Don't get so close—you're crushing my lilacs." "What a great day it is!" "Oh! One o'clock already. I wonder how Uncle Julio is doing. He's always in such a hurry to have lunch." With this kind of talk they covered up being embarrassed, not at the kind act, but at the error or sentimental disappointment that had prompted it.

Little by little the streetcar was emptying. At the intersection of Goya Street many people got off. They did so quickly, like someone who sheds a burden or puts an end to an embarrassing situation, and avoided looking at the woman who sat quietly in her corner, ever tremulous, and allowing her momentary benefactors to leave without even saying to them: "God bless you." Did she notice that the streetcar was practically deserted? I couldn't help but call it to her attention.

"Where are you going? Look, we're approaching the end of the line. Don't get distracted and go past your house."

I got no response from her either, but with a weary shake of the head she clearly expressed to me: 'You serious? I have a long way to go. God knows how far I'll walk after the last stop.'

The devil (who also gets involved occasionally in these mercy matters) tempted me to determine if words would improve on money in soothing somewhat the ulceration of that raw spirit.

"Take heart, woman," I said to her energetically. "If your husband is a wicked man, don't you get discouraged because of it. You have a little boy in your arms . . . you ought to work and live for him. For this child you ought to attempt what you wouldn't attempt on your own behalf. One of these days the boy will learn a trade and be your refuge. Mothers don't have a right to give in to despair while their children are alive."

This time the woman came out of her stupor; she turned and faced me with dry, inflamed eyes hooded by ghastly, droopy, bloodshot eyelids. It was a stare to shake the soul. The child, meanwhile, had awakened and stretched his little arms, yawning lazily. And the woman, picking him up and holding him in the air, showed him to me. Sunshine lit up his whole face and his wide-open eyes. Wide-open, but white, coagulated, and motionless. The forsaken woman's son was blind.

The Gravedigger*

The most beautiful girl in the little town of Arfe had a name as pretty as her face. It was Pura, and her neighbors had reinforced the symbolism of it by always calling her Puri la Casta.* This appellation, suggestive of a white lily, harmonized perfectly with her type: fair skin, fresh complexion, and blonde hair. She was also innocent-looking to the point of being somewhat dull, a common defect in small town beauties, in whom coquetry is immediately characterized as fickleness, and talent and malice would pass, if they existed, for profound depravity. In the region of Spain where Arfe is located, a woman is required to be devout, faithful, home-loving, strong, free from affectation, and, for greater assurance, a little on the cool side. So it was with La Casta—a shut garden, a sealed-off fountain from which flowed only limpid water. Because of her demeanor and because of her shapely figure, young men of all social classes pursued her with ardor, and elderly men held her in an affectionate regard, greater and more justified than the admiration that the old men of Troy had for Helen,* wife of Menelaus.

La Casta did not, however, make of her maidenhood an offering to God, for which reason she had numerous suitors; and as soon as one of honorable background and intentions appeared, a youth of pure blood and comfortable means, she consented to being courted. She responded to his proposal with an honest yes, and since among such people and in such areas the yes is tantamount to a sacred commitment, the probable duration of the engagement and approximate date of the marriage were agreed to at once. The engagement passed quickly, a mixture of amorous conversations, innocent courtesies, and permissible pleasures, without the fiancé—a young man of tender feelings and highly noble character—ever attempting to seek, as a pledge of the arranged nuptials, even the slightest foretaste of future delights. Not because the fever of desire didn't excite his passion, nor because he didn't dream every night of the joy of pulling the petals off the untouched white lily one by one, breathing its perfume, but because in his fiancée he respected his wife-to-be, and the cloth that covered her statuesque beauty was as sacred to him as the trim of the Virgin's cloak.

Nevertheless, as the wedding day drew near, the passion of Puri's fiancé was running high and it was becoming increasingly more difficult for him not to show with some intensity his rapture. For her part, the beautiful Puri was considerably more expansive with her future husband, and because the nearness of the wedding ceremony set her at ease, she had no qualms about approaching and talking to him with greater familiarity and affectionate trust. So it was that on a certain afternoon, as the engaged couple chatted in the courtyard of Puri's house, her fiancé could no longer control himself, and, grabbing her by the waist, he held her tightly and kissed her in a frenzy—roughly and by fits and starts—about the hair and forehead. No sooner had he vented his desire than he felt remorse and shame, while Puri, pale and frowning, stepped backward, looking at him in astonishment, almost in fear. The lovesick fiancé straightened his shoulders, mumbled a few incomprehensible phrases and fled, angry with himself, and accusing himself of a moral desecration, as untimely as it was foolish.

The following day, on seeing La Casta pale, downcast, and melancholy, his anxiety increased. He immediately believed her condition to be a consequence of his excess, but Puri dispelled his fears by assuring him repeatedly that it was nothing more than physical discomfort, a minor indisposition, the kind that can't be pinpointed because the whole body feels its effects. The following morning, the discomfort, far from disappearing, turned into a real ailment that forced Puri to stay in bed. And the girl never again got up from her bed except to be carried from it by four bearers to Arfe's cemetery.

The fiancé's understandable bitterness took on a somber, frantic edge akin to madness. There were no words of consolation for him; he refused to eat; he no sooner laughed than he bellowed with rage or tore at his hair, biting his hands in desperation. No matter how much the doctor assured him again and again that Puri had died from a very common, natural illness—acute cerebral fever—the poor devil persisted in assuming that his boldness had occasioned the death of that lovely, robust creature. The fateful 'I killed her,' a confused, inarticulate feeling, sprang up from the bottom of his conscience, darkening his spirit with pessimism and the gloom of alienation. Ashen, and staring aimlessly at an invisible point in space as he mumbled prayers with his hands convulsively interlocked, he stayed at the dead Puri's bedside and then accompanied her to her final resting place. Dressed in blue and white—the habit of the nuns of the Immaculate Conception; barely ravaged by the fever; her beautiful blonde hair loose and framing her peaceful face, fresh in appearance in spite of death; and with the virgins' palm over her breast, Puri la Casta went to her grave in a state of incredible beauty, more striking than in life, if that's conceivable.

This was the opinion of the neighbor women and girl friends who escorted her on her final journey, and the gravedigger, old Carmelo, concurred with that special, funereal laughter of his that curdled the blood. Old Carmelo was a little man in his fifties with a lean, cynical face, the kind seen on skeletons which, as is well-known, are always laughing—in their own way. Shriveled and dried up like a piece of tinder, with bright, colorless eyes and a bald, shiny pate, continuous laughter revealed his yellow teeth; and joy, which in the rest of men is usually a sign of benevolence and a friendly, healthy disposition, in him was like a sinister light that illuminates a grave. If the inhabitants of Arfe read Shakespeare, they would remember a certain scene from *Hamlet* when they caught sight of the gravedigger with his morbid laughter and banter about life beyond the grave, and Puri, laid out in her coffin, would evoke the image of Ophelia.*

Old Carmelo was the son and grandson of gravediggers, but the line ended with him because the girls from Arfe and the surrounding towns refused to cast their lot with the ugly, sarcastic burial man. The pain of loneliness had probably embittered Carmelo's youth, but from the time that he reached maturity he seemed so completely resigned to his fate that his gibes, sneers, and taunts were usually about husbands, boyfriends, and fiancés. He scoffed at them, having the effrontery to say that their fiancées and wives had been or would be unfaithful to them—all of them, without exception—some time; only the sheer general nature of

the jest made it tolerable, for if the men of Arfe believed that the
gravedigger spoke in earnest and was alluding to one of them in
particular, their response would have been to pull his venomous
tongue out of his mouth. His coarse and somewhat loose remarks,
his jokes in bad taste, and his continuous snicker—jeering and
insulting—were tolerated, because the touch of contempt for his
profession, redounded on the man, and towns, like monarchs,
do not derive their legitimacy from the malicious gossip of the
miserable jester. Besides, the Arfenians, decent people of good-
will, felt sorry for that old man who dwelled among the deceased, in total abandonment and solitude, with no human
attachment to gladden his heart, no gentle touch in his dreary
life as a fifty-year old. Nothing positively bad was known about
him; he earned a living by the sweat of his brow, and the very
horror of his occupation aroused greater sympathy.

The unfortunate Puri was left in the hands of the unpleasant
old man after they had closed and lowered the casket into the
pit and dumped on it the shovelfuls of earth that were to cover
it. Her fiancé did not jump into the grave like Hamlet the Dane
to talk nonsense and make philosophical boasts—he was too
much of a Christian to commit such an atrocity. But while the
prayers for the dead were sung and the priest sprinkled the dead
girl's pretty face with holy water, while the casket was covered
and earth shoveled to fill in the excavation, the future husband
stood there staring at the divine features that the grave's worms
were going to contest and listened to the muffled noise of the
shovels, lost in thought and numb with pain. After the ground
was leveled, he turned around and, without shedding a tear or
uttering a sigh, he withdrew, giving the impression of a harmless
lunatic who moves away from sane people to meditate freely.

He remained shut up inside his house until nightfall, which
descended on the small town like a soft cloak of dark velvet
studded with glittering lights, for it was the month of May and
the firmament's calm harmonized with the pulsation of the ger-
minating earth. No sooner had darkness fallen on Arfe, than
Puri's fiancé, raising his head and resting his index finger on his
forehead, shuddered. He felt overcome by the lugubrious notion
that his loved one would be all alone in the cemetery, and believed that the right thing to do was to accompany her for a while

and pray over her recently filled-in grave. Such an intention brought on relief; without knowing why, his chest expanded, drawing him out of the terrible absorption and stillness of grief, for which any resolve, any activity, provides alleviation. He wrapped himself in his cape—from instinct and habit, because rather than cold he felt the heat of a fever—took his hat, and set out for the cemetery along out-of-the-way streets.

Arfe is situated on the slope of a little mountain range, with the houses spread out on its incline. The circuit of the cemetery's walls follows the same slant, so that at the high point they're very easy to climb, especially for someone who has the agility of youth and knows how to catch hold of the bushes and stones. Puri's fiancé got inside the enclosure with little difficulty, and if his heart had not been throbbing with a sacred emotion, the fatigue of the ascent wouldn't have been sufficient to make it beat faster.

To gain access, he chose a somewhat run-down bend in the wall where a dense clump of cypresses cast its long pyramidal shadow on the ground; two olive trees added to its reach. In spite of the brightness of the new moon, at first it was difficult for him to get his bearings. He knew that the grave was behind another clump of trees, in a corner where there were few crosses, a kind of preferential location more solitary and distinguished than the others. Finally, Puri's fiancé found the way.

From the moment that he got inside the cemetery to say farewell to his intended like the inamorato of Venice,* he felt, without understanding the reason, a dread, a coldness, a feverish chill, a sensation that made his heart pound and brought a lump to his throat and paralyzed his legs. Motionless before the handful of trees, a curtain for Puri's deathbed, he trembled as if fright, widespread and invisible to the eyes of mortal man, were going to rise from her grave. Would he dare to cover the distance and enter the mysterious corner where darkness was intensified and religious terror hovered in attendance? Behind those trees was his fiancée, to be sure, but not like always—beautiful, proud, rose-colored, and crowned with golden tresses; on the contrary, she was livid, stiff, laid out, her hands crossed over the palm of her virginity. The Catholic youth, feeling a divine swell in his soul and tears of faith in his eyes, got ready to kneel at the grave and pray for his dead fiancée . . . or to his dead fiancée, to her angelical spirit, that perhaps was floating there, in the tepid atmosphere of the May night.

Was it a trick of the imagination? Was it hallucination brought on by suffering? He would swear that he heard a sound behind the clump of trees, the sound of breathing, odd and out of place for the august silence appropriate to such a setting at such an hour. Irrational uneasiness and apprehension restored to the heartbroken fiancé his consciousness of reality and defensive reaction, and like a thrown dart he rushed frantically toward the grave. The most profound horror, the most frightful rage, powerful enough to freeze his will and restrain his arm when they ought to have driven him to pounce like the avenging hand of God, prevented him from tearing into pieces on the very spot the infamous gravedigger, who in that corner of the cemetery was perpetrating an unspeakable crime with the exhumed, stiff, white, and beautiful body of Puri la Casta.

When old Carmelo, his hands tied behind his back, appeared before the judge—after passing through the crowd that was in a drunken fury, in a lynching mood, and shouting in a loud voice to be allowed to parade the gravedigger in a pannier—far from being humble, contrite, downcast or full of confusion, he was undaunted, sarcastic, smiling, showing off as never before the funereal humor that characterized him. When the law's representative rebuked him for his hideous desecration, Carmelo, instead of showing remorse, of attributing the act to momentary aberration or frenzy that obliterated reason and conscience, raised his head, made a face of defiance and scorn, spoke in a firm voice with the stridence of a whistle, and the whole town of Arfe, that decent, Christian, law-abiding town, jealous of a good name more than esteem, that makes of honor a principle and reputation a shrine—the whole town of Arfe, I repeat, learned that the lowest of men (if there weren't an executioner), a loathsome little old man, disgrace and scum of humanity, had affronted them continuously in the persons of their mothers, wives, sisters, and daughters, for a period of thirty-some years, deliberately and without risk.

A nauseating tragedy! Nobody escaped the posthumous slap in the face from those contemptible fingers—the outrage that is

neither avoided nor punished, the stain that isn't washed away
with all the water of the River Jordan. For that cemetery Tarquinius there existed no Lucrecia;* his fierceness destroyed the notion of virtue and established equality in the Arfenians' lives
before shame and dishonor. The crowd, which earlier was ranting
and raging and wanted to take the law in its own hands, had
become subdued, stunned by the very magnitude of the offense
and the appalling cynicism of the one who confessed to it. The
assembled townspeople listened to him in silence as he poured
a stream of vile abuse on them. The judge himself was at a loss
and—strange weakness!—flagged when bringing charges. So that
the reader won't be surprised by some of the expressions drawn
from old Carmelo's testimony in the excerpt of dialogue that I'm
going to transcribe, I should point out that the town of Arfe (very
real indeed, and shown on the map, although under a different
name), has an independent secondary school, founded by a
wealthy Arfenian, which provides a free and very comprehensive
education to the inhabitants of the little mountain town, and that
the gravedigger, as a youngster, had studied there.

Judge. Didn't putting your hands on a dead person make you
shudder?
Accused. I was born in the midst of dead people. My father was a
gravedigger, my grandfather was one, and I guess my great-
grandfather was too. For me there's no difference between the living
and the dead. How do you expect my clientele to revolt me or make
me shudder if I cut my teeth handling and touching corpses?
Judge. Doesn't the coldness of the skin, the rigor mortis, have a
depressing effect on you? What attraction can a dead body have?
Accused. Colder and more insensitive than the women I bury are
some of the live ones loved by the men of this town.
Judge. Hold your tongue. How long have you been committing
these horrible desecrations, you wretch?
Accused. Since I became persuaded that no girl in the town would
give me the time of day; since my flattery became their amusement
and my proposals their farce; since my job made me a laughingstock
and my person a bogeyman. Since the town feast day when I couldn't
find a dance partner. Well, the dance that I had later on with those
prim women wasn't bad at all!
Judge. Stop! You're a monster, an affront to the human race!
Accused. Some piece of news! That's why I've taken revenge on
everybody. I committed wrongs for the very reason that I am a monster. I've been convicted and admit my guilt. And hear this, Your

Honor, to keep things clear and in their proper place: I also want it known that I've never so much as taken a nickel's worth of what the dead women wore to their graves. Let the coffins be opened and where they should be you'll find rings, earrings, and lockets. I'm no thief.

Judge. You've stolen something infinitely more valuable, decency and dignity.

Accused. If dignity and decency don't depend on the will of the person in question, and can be taken away like that . . . as I've taken them, then I admit that I have unquestionably dishonored the inhabitants of Arfe. *(A pervasive murmur among the onlookers. Threats and curses, silenced by the grisly curiosity of wanting to hear.)*

Judge. Temper your language. Your insolence will aggravate the severity of the law and make inexorable the sentence pronounced by the court. Apparent in you, besides the pattern of such brutal assaults, is a rancorous spirit and the hatred of a field. Evil man, what harm did the people of the peaceful town of Arfe cause you?

Accused. Harm? Not much. Just treat me like a dog. Example: even if a girl loved me, her father wouldn't let me marry her. He'd sooner see her wed to a highwayman. They refused to let me have a single one of their daughters! Well, I had all of them, and as much as I wanted to, without having to woo them or walk up and down the streets where they lived. I said it openly to the men of Arfe, and they were determined to pay me no heed: "There isn't a man in this town whose wife hasn't been unfaithful to him at least once." And the great big oafs laughed. They laughed. Don't all of you cry out . . . Now you'll believe that old Carmelo never lies. Well, and what about the ones who died before marrying and came clutching their palms, like this, and their fiancés didn't even dare touch the hems of their skirts? The girl brought in the other night was like that. . . Mind you, she was a good-looking one, Your Honor! And they called her Puri la Casta . . . Ha-ha!

Carmelo's infamous guffaw was greeted by an anguished sob and then a howl as the townspeople flung themselves at the abominable transgressor. Puri's fiancé all of a sudden fell to the ground, like a stone that breaks loose from the mountain and rolls, lifelessly and noiselessly, to the plain.

For a year the pitiful young man was half mad, engaging in all kinds of behavior, from despondent to furious. Upon recovering his sanity, he entered as a novice the Franciscan monastery which had just been started up again in Priego.

Don Juan's Last Illusion

Superficial people who have never taken the trouble to observe closely the complicated mechanism of the heart, freely suppose that Don Juan, the precocious libertine, the sempiternal seducer, is content with enjoyment of the senses and, at most, fantasy; and they believe that he neither needs nor indulges in the useless luxury of sentiment, and that he never opens the gilded window of contemplation where the spirit appears to look out at the sky when the weightiness of earth oppresses him. I tell you truly that these superficial people are altogether mistaken and unfair to poor Don Juan, whom only we poets have understood, we who are awash with charity and are perceptive . . . precisely because, although naive in appearance, we believe in many things.

To make the truth known, I'm going to tell you the story of how Don Juan nourished and maintained his last illusion . . . and how he came to lose it.

Among the numerous relations of Don Juan—who, let it be said in passing, is a nobleman like the king—are several female cousins, widely celebrated for their beauty, who live out in the country. The youngest, Estrella, differed from her sisters in her gentleness of character, exaltation of virtue, and religious fervor, for which reason at home she was called "the little saint." Her angelical face did not belie the qualities of her soul: she looked like one of Murillo's Virgins, of the kind who exude chastity and purity (because some, like the brunette "of the napkin," called *Refitolera,** only exude youth and vigor). Whenever Don Juan's vagabond mood prompted him to take a trip through the region where his cousins lived, he would go to see them, frequent their company, and hold endless talks with Estrella. If you ask me what magnet drew the rake to the saint, and what's even more, her to him, I'll tell you that perhaps it was the very contrast of their temperaments, and after this explanation we'll know as much as we did before.

The fact is that while Don Juan courted all women as a matter of course, with Estrella he talked seriously, not allowing himself the slightest disrespectful insinuation; and while Estrella shunned dealings with all men, she approached Don Juan's hand like the gentle, trusting dove, certain of not soiling its white plumage. The whole world was free to listen to the cousins' conversations, and after hours of agreeable, restful, and innocuous talk, they would stand up so self-possessed, and calm and happy, and Estrella would rush off to the kitchen or pantry to prepare carefully one of the dishes that she knew pleased Don Juan. More than the treats, he savored the loving attention with which they were served, and his cousin's youthful vitality and sedative effect soothed him like a cooling bath for one who has walked a long time over scorching sandy terrain.

When Don Juan departed, going off to big cities where life is feverish excitement and lunacy, Estrella would write him long, rambling letters, and he would answer with a few lines—but he would always answer. On returning home at dawn, staggering and dazed by the bacchanalia or still throbbing with excitement from the violent emotions of the tryst; on shutting himself in to swallow, in the middle of an ironic laugh, the bitter pill of disappointment—because Don Juan also experiences them; on preparing himself for an affair of honor, tempering his will to face death fearlessly; on laughing and blaspheming; and on depriving his youth and health like a prodigal fool of the most valued possessions with which we are blessed, Don Juan reserved and set aside—as money is set aside for an offering to Our Lady—ten minutes to be devoted to Estrella. In his quest for love, that chaste dedication to such a noble and refined being represented the sip of water that is drunk in the middle of battle and restores strength to the combatant to continue fighting. The treachery, duplicity, perfidy, and infamy of other women could be borne with patience, as long as in a corner of the world he inspired the loyal affection of Estrella, "the little saint." With each ingenuous and enchanting letter that he received, Don Juan had the same dream: he saw himself walking with effort through a very dense, cold, and almost palpable darkness which was broken at intervals by the sulfurous flash of lightning and the zigzag of thunderbolts. But in the distance, a long way off, where the sky was clearing up, Don Juan made out a white, veiled figure, a woman with downcast eyes, holding a small, lighted lamp in her right hand and shielding it with her left. That light was never extinguished.

The years were, in effect, passing quickly. Don Juan was plunging headlong down the path of his delirium and the letters continued to arrive with unalterable regularity, full of the same latent, serene tenderness. So pleasing were these letters to Don Juan that he had determined not to see his cousin again, fearful of finding her less attractive and changed by time, and then no longer having sufficient illusion to maintain the correspondence. At any price he wished to perpetuate his daydream, to see Estrella always with the Murillo-like face, the twenty-year-old virgin saint. Don Juan's letters, in truth, expressed an intense desire to visit his cousin, to renew the pleasant chats, but since nobody was preventing Don Juan from carrying out this intention, one has to conclude—because the trip was not being undertaken— that the desire was not terribly pressing.

Ten years had gone by when one day Don Juan received, in place of the usual wide double sheet, written on all four sides and signed, a brief, unsigned note, serious and reserved in style, and in which even the handwriting lacked the abandon that imparts effusion of spirit by guiding the hand and making it caress, so to speak, the paper. Oh, woman! Oh, running water! Oh, fleeting flame! Oh, breath of air! Estrella asked Don Juan not to be surprised and not to become angry, and confessed to him that she was going to get married soon . . . An ideal fiancé had turned up, a wonderful man, honest and rich, to whom Estrella's father owed countless favors. Everybody's counsel and encouragement had persuaded the little saint, who hoped—with God's help—to gain salvation.

Don Juan was left momentarily absorbed in thought; then he crumpled the paper and threw it scornfully at the lighted chimney. To think that if someone had told him a few hours ago that Estrella could marry, he would have called such a person a contemptible liar! And she herself was informing him, unashamedly, like somebody who's telling the most natural and permissible thing in the world!

Since that day Don Juan, the gay libertine, has lost his last illusion, and his soul is wandering in the shadows, without ever seeing the glimmer of the soft lamp that a virgin shields with her hand. The man who still had something of a human being about him is only a wild beast, with teeth to seize and claws to destroy mercilessly. His profession of faith is a cynical burst of laughter, and his love a whiplash that sears and tears away skin causing blood to gush forth . . .

You'll say to me that the little saint had a right to seek real happiness and pleasures even more pure than those that her wanton idol imbibed without respite. And most likely you're right, according to popular common sense and petty, practical, minor considerations. May such feeble reasoning stand you in good stead! In the opinion of poets, being a captive of vice is preferable to being a deserter of the ideal. The little saint sinned against poetry and against the divine dreams of unattainable love. Don Juan, believing in eternal abnegation, was, of the two, the true dreamer.

The Guilty Woman

Elisa was very unhappy throughout her married life, and died still a young woman, sapped by grief. It's true that she had made a very grave mistake, so grave that for her there was no forgiveness: running away with the man who had not yet become her husband and spending twenty-four hours with him on a train. Afterwards the usual happened; the police picked her up, took her to a convent, and two weeks later she got married. Her parents didn't attend the wedding, a very proper response in the opinion of sensible people.

The mother and father hadn't opposed Elisa and Adolfo's courtship openly, but inasmuch as they were not at all pleased with the suitor and believed that they knew what he was like, and had a premonition of his moral makeup, they created a thousand petty obstacles and succeeded in delaying the matter and keeping them waiting for a period of five years. Of course, they permitted Adolfo to enter their home because he had little of the seducer in him and was even unpleasant, and they hoped that Elisa's dreams would vanish on seeing him close up. Just the opposite happened: in the interminable conversations next to the fireplace, in the daily cooing of the two lovebirds, Elisa's enamored heart succumbed forever, and Adolfo secured his capture of the affluent young woman. Following well-planned and strategic maneuvers on the part of the fiancé, the moment of the elopement—the preliminary to marriage—arrived.

Elisa's family took the scandal very much to heart for the very reason that they were well-known, well-connected, and considered very proper and uncompromising in matters of outward morality. The household went through one of those solemn, profound periods of reserved trial during which even the servants are depressed; periods that inch people who are getting on in years closer to the grave. The fugitive's two sisters were ashamed

and embarrassed to such an extent that for many months they
didn't dare to leave the house. One in particular was so upset
that she had to be moved from Madrid to preserve her health.
The mother never said Elisa's name without crying, as when one
mentions the dead. The father carried the reaction to extremes—
he was adamant and never mentioned Elisa at all. If he was asked
how many daughters he had, he said two. "I lost the other one,"
he would say, twitching his lips.

Married now to the man she had chosen, Elisa determined to
live beyond reproach and be perfect in everything to atone for
her mistake. There was no wife more loving and solicitous than
Elisa, no house better managed than hers, no woman who did
without with greater self-denial and faded more modestly into
the obscurity of the home. Because she was after all still quite
young and at times blood bubbled in her veins with youthful
energy, when she saw other married women dress up, deck themselves with jewels, go to dances and parties and smile at the
mirror while she was confined to the house in a dressing gown,
she would say to herself: "Fine, but they didn't run away with
their husbands before the wedding." And even if she learned
that they ran off afterwards or did something similar, with other
men, she always persisted in considering them to be of superior
character.

Elisa saw herself as having to justify her behavior to such an
extent that she never went out alone, nor did she permit visitors
if her husband wasn't home. She spoke to all men, whether they
were young or old, coldly and curtly, cutting conversation immediately. She wore dark dresses that covered her from the neck
down and her hairdo was by design plain and simple. Fond of
perfumes and eau de cologne, Elisa abolished them completely
from the time she heard that "the honest woman should smell
neither good nor bad." To be regarded as an honest woman was
her ambition and her dream, but she had little hope of ever
achieving it because of that business of the runaway.

After the brief honeymoon was over, Adolfo began to go astray,
and using politics as a pretext, he got in the habit of going to bed
late and spending his days outside the home, not returning even
to eat. Elisa cried in silence—she cried a great deal because she

loved him, she loved him with all her heart, and couldn't live happily except with him and for him, the man for whom she had sacrificed everything.

One day, searching through her husband's clothes closet to clean or arrange his clothing, she found, forgotten in a summer morning coat, a letter that left no doubt. The pain was so sharp that Elisa got in bed and spent several days not wanting to eat but very much wanting to die. As soon as she plucked up a bit of courage, she got out of bed and went on living. She didn't utter a single complaint. With what right? She could be silenced after two or three words. And what if the elopement was brought up?

Children came, a boy and a girl, but Elisa, on whom all the burden of their upbringing fell, did not have a hand in their education, nor did she ever exercise that authority of the proud, dignified mother who wears her motherhood like a crown. Her children grew used to the fact that "Mama didn't give the orders."

As for finances, the clear inference is that they were controlled solely and exclusively by Adolfo, and Elisa would not have plunged into spending fifty *pesetas* on anything unusual without the necessary consent. After her father died and she received her rightful share of the estate, which was still substantial although reduced as a result of paternal anger, Adolfo took charge of all of it and spent the major portion for his own enjoyment, not without Elisa frequently hearing harsh reproaches and bitter allusions, based on the notion that her father had disinherited her or close to it.

Elisa's health suffered. The doctors spoke of lesions in the heart that were degenerating into dropsy. Since her condition worsened, she asked for a priest and for the hundredth time confessed her offense: the disastrous runaway. The priest instructed her to confess her present-day sins because God is not in the habit of recounting the ones that are already forgiven and absolved. But Heaven's absolution wasn't enough for Elisa. Everyone knows that God is very benevolent, but man, on the other hand, never forgets certain things, and the strain of shame is there, on the forehead, until the final minute of life.

With her eyes glazed by tears, Elisa asked for Adolfo to come, and as soon as she saw him at her headboard, she threw her arms around his neck and mumbled in his ear: "My love, my darling, I know I have no right to ask that you . . . that you not remarry . . . but at least . . . look, at this moment of my death . . . forgive me sincerely for that business . . . and don't forget me like this . . . so quickly . . . so quickly."

Adolfo didn't respond; nevertheless, it seemed natural to him to bend down and kiss her. And the guilty woman, letting her head fall on the pillow, died happy.

The Faithful Fiancée

The breakup of the engagement of Germán Riaza and Amelia Sirvián came as a big surprise to all of Marineda; the separation of a married couple doesn't give rise to as much commentary. People had become accustomed to believing that their marriage was a foregone conclusion and nobody understood what caused the rupture, not even the fiancé. Only Amelia's confessor learned the key to the puzzle.

What's certain is that their engagement was dragging on for so long that it had almost amounted to an institution. Ten years of betrothal is no small matter. Amelia became Germán's fiancée at the first dance she attended after her coming-out.

And how pretty she looked at that dance! She wore a white crepe dress cut just low enough in front to reveal the beginning of her virginal shoulders and bosom, which was heaving with excitement and pleasure, while withering rosebuds adorned her powdered blonde hair. Amelia was, in the opinion of a group of elderly women, a "colored print," an "engraving" from *La Ilustración*. Germán asked her to dance, and when he squeezed her supple waist and felt the freshness of her innocent breath, he lost his head; agitated and not attempting to choose his words carefully, he made an ardent proposal in a shaking voice and was rewarded with a spontaneous *Yes* that came out half involuntarily and was, therefore, doubly delightful. From the following day they wrote to each other, and then came that period—conversations at Amelia's window and pursuit in the streets—which is like the dawn of true romance. Neither Amelia's parents, who were modest proprietors, nor Germán's, fairly well-to-do merchants but with a large family, objected to the young couple's wish, taking for granted from the outset that it would culminate in a proper marriage as soon as Germán completed his law studies and could assume the responsibilities of a family.

The first six years were delightful. Germán spent the winters in

Compostela, studying at the university and writing long, tender missives; with reading them, rereading them, answering them, and anxiously awaiting summer vacations, time slipped by imperceptibly for Amelia. The vacation periods were pleasing intervals and Amelia knew that her fiancé would devote himself totally to her while they lasted. Germán was still not received in the house, but he accompanied Amelia on walks, and at night they talked, by the light of the moon, near a balcony with a view of the sea. His absences, broken up by frequent returns, were almost a lure, an added delight, a continuous fascination, something that filled Amelia's existence and left no room for sadness or ennui.

As soon as Germán had his law degree in his pocket, he decided to go to Madrid to study for the doctorate. A year of trial for the fiancée! Germán hardly wrote—just notes scribbled on the run, probably on a café table, that were brief, dull, and lacking in affection. And her concerned girl friends, who saw a worried and listless Amelia with rings under her eyes, said to her with teasing disloyalty:

"Come on, silly, have some fun. Lord knows what he's doing there! You're a fool if you think he's not cheating on you! My cousin Lorenzo wrote to me that he saw Germán in high spirits at the theater with a 'couple of . . .'"

The joy of Germán's return compensated for these sorrows. Two days later Amelia no longered remembered her suffering, her doubts, her suspicions. And Germán, having been given permission to enter his fiancée's home, now came every night when the family gathered for conversation, and in the semi-darkness of the corner where the piano stood, far from the oil lamp covered with a silk shade, the engaged couple talked endlessly, from time to time searching for each other's hands to exchange a furtive squeeze, their eyes always locked to explore the depths of their love.

Never had Amelia been so happy. What more could she desire? Germán was there, and the wedding was an agreed upon and resolved matter, postponed only out of the necessity of Germán's finding himself a modest position in, say, the public prosecutor's office. But when another year had passed and still no position had been found, Germán decided to open a law office and get involved in local politics to see if he could gain favor and obtain the coveted job. His new responsibilities forced him to see Amelia less frequently and to spend less time with her when he did. When she complained of the change, Germán defended himself at length saying it was necessary to think of the future; Amelia knew perfectly well that one of these days they would get married, and she shouldn't attach importance to minor matters and indulge in affectations characteristic of people who are beginning to think only about themselves. Germán continued, in effect, with the firm intention of getting married as soon as circumstances permitted.

By the ninth year of the engagement Amelia's parents (as well as everybody else) noticed that the girl's character seemed completely altered. Instead of the wholesome gaiety and evenness of disposition that graced her personality, she appeared to be driven by peculiarities and caprices, first roaring with laughter, then maintaining a sullen silence. Her health also changed for the worse. She became aware of an insurmountable loss of appetite; she experienced unbearable insomnia that forced her to spend nights out of bed because, as she explained, when she lay awake it seemed like her tomb; and she suffered, moreover, from heartache and nervous attacks. When asked the cause of her malaise she would answer laconically, "I don't know." And that was true, but in the end she did discover what it was, and discovering it caused her greater harm.

What minimal signs, what hidden but related facts, what unexplainable revelations that emerge from the world around us cause yesterday's innocent virgin—without her learning anything new or concrete, without anybody informing her with immodest exactness—to understand unexpectedly and tear the veil of Isis* from her eyes? Amelia, all of a sudden, understood. Her malaise was none other than desire, longing, urgency, the need to marry. What shame, what blushing, what grief and what disillusionment if Germán even came to suspect it! Oh! She would rather die first! Hide it, hide it at all costs, so that neither fiancé nor parents nor the world would know!

On seeing Germán so calm, so self-assured, so armed with patience, and gaining weight while she was wasting away; on seeing him jovial while she soaked her pillow with tears, Amelia chastised herself and admired her fiancé's serenity, prudence, and virtue. And in order to control herself and not fling herself in his arms sobbing, in order not to carry out the unspeakable madness of going out alone one afternoon and calling on Germán, Amelia needed all her courage, all her circumspection, and all the restraint of the notions of honor and decency that had been inculcated in her since childhood.

One day, without knowing how, without an extraordinary event or overhead conversation to enlighten her, the last threads of the veil were torn away. Amelia saw the light; the terrible notion of reality burned in the depths of her being. Upon remembering that shortly before she had admired Germán's resignation and envied his patience, and understanding now the true reason for that incomparable patience and resignation, a sardonic peal of laughter spread her lips while she thought she felt in her throat a slipknot that was tightening little by little and strangling her. The convulsion was horrible, and long, and unyielding, and as soon as the shattered Amelia was able to react, to recover, to talk ... she implored her parents to notify Germán that the engagement was broken. Letters from her fiancé, entreaties, parental advice—it was all in vain. Amelia clung to her decision and persisted in it without giving reasons or excuses.

"Child, to my way of thinking, you've made a big mistake," Fr. Incienso was saying to her as she knelt at the foot of the confessional, her face awash with tears. "A reliable and hardworking young man, disposed to marry—you don't find his kind easily. Even waiting to have a position before starting a family I consider laudable. As for the rest of it ... those figments of your imagination ... Men, unfortunately ... While single he's probably enjoyed those diversions ... But, you ..."

"Father," the young woman exclaimed, "believe me, because I'm talking to God here. I loved him ... I still love him ... and because I do, because I do, Father! If I don't leave him ... I'll imitate him! I too will ... !"

Christ's Thirst

When Christ opened His desiccated mouth and uttered the most anguished of the Seven Words from the height of His gallows, Mary Magdalene, who appeared crazed with grief, shuddered while wrapped around the cross in a tight embrace; recovering energy and movement and driven by a compassion that penetrated her entire being, she dashed off in search of water to quench the dying Teacher's thirst.

Magdalene knew that an unadulterated and limpid spring flowed between large rocks not very far from Calvary. She borrowed a clay cup from a Jerusalem man, one of those who surrounded the cross en masse, and set out for the secluded fountain. It didn't take her long to find it, and she felt profound elation thinking that a drink of the pure, pellucid water would relieve, at least momentarily, the Martyr's suffering. The steady stream, more transparent than glass, gushed from a crevice blanketed with moss and delicate ferns, and the murmur of its flow gladdened the ear and heart. On filling the earthenware vessel with water, Magdalene noticed that it was very cold, almost gelid, and experienced joy anew thinking about how refreshing the sip would be for Jesus. With her cup overflowing she ran to the site of Christ's ordeal, and by dint of supplication succeeded in obtaining permission from the executioners to stack a few stones and climb them until bringing the water close to the crucified Lord's purple lips. When she expected to see Him savor the consoling water, behold—Jesus refused it, moving his head and repeating in an imperceptible voice: "I'm thirsty."

With the insight of love—because in truth I say to you that there is nothing that enlightens a woman's comprehension like loving a good deal and in earnest—Magdalene guessed that Christ desired another drink more exquisite and rare than natural water, and it was imperative to bring it to Him whatever the cost. While she rushed toward Jerusalem she remembered that

72

the steward and butler of the tetrarch Herod had treated her long ago to a very mellow Falernian wine, hot like fire and sweet like honey, a single drop of which is capable of reviving a stiff corpse. Hastily and imploringly, the repentant sinner pleaded with her former suitor, and inasmuch as he acceded to her entreaties, she returned to Calvary radiant with anticipation, hiding underneath her cloak the amphora of incalculable value, and held the spout to Jesus' lips. A more pronounced gesture of repugnance and a weak moan that made the pitiful "I'm thirsty" barely audible demonstrated to Magdalene that she still did not possess the means of relieving the holy Victim's agony.

In her grief and anger with herself for not having guessed correctly, the memory of her licentious youth flashed vividly across Magdalene's mind. She remembered clearly that a Roman patrician—a pompous epicurean, reader of Horace and something of a poet himself—who did hundreds of crazy things for her, the beautiful daughter of Jerusalem, used to talk about the feasts of the pagan Olympus and the mysterious power and incomparable essence of the gods' nectar, which instills happiness and injects life in massive doses into exhausted veins and exanimate bodies. And as if some secret evil power—perhaps Satan's, determined to the end to tempt the Redeemer to prove His divinity—were an accomplice to the sinner's senseless longing, she felt herself swept away and transported with incredible speed on wings of the wind, which gently set her down on the summit of a delightful mountain filled with olives, laurels, and blossom-laden orange trees that mixed with thickets of myrtle and flowering rosebushes that emitted an intoxicating perfume. Gracefully descending the staircase of an elegant white marble pavilion, there came to meet Magdalene a handsome, smiling youth who had glittering pupils and curly hair the color of jacinth, and he presented to her an exquisitely engraved gold krater wherein sparkled a pink, transparent liqueur with an intoxicating fragrance that dazed the senses. Full of joy, Magdalene squeezed the sacred ambrosia against her breast and thought of nothing now except offering it to Jesus, because it was impossible that that glorious liqueur, served by Ganymede,* not stir the Martyr's spirit, making Him forget His suffering. Just by carrying the cup of ambrosia in her hands Magdalene felt herself gripped by a mild fever and ecstasy, and nature seemed more beautiful to her—the sun brighter, and the air lighter, more buoyant, and more luminous. Bitter disappointment! As soon as she could bring a cup overflowing with ambrosia close to the lips of the moribund Redeemer, whose tendons were bursting and whose face was distorted from horrible suffering, Jesus made a gesture of violent repulsion, and liqueur and cup tumbled to the ground, spilling the drink of the pagan gods over the dry earth.

Magdalene, a victim of temptation, then felt her bitterness intensify. The vices of her years of iniquity reappeared, because sin leaves sediments in the soul and rises to the surface as soon as it is stirred by passion, and although Christ's teachings had inflamed this woman's spirit, it was still necessary for her to do penance to be purified and to destroy the old leavening. It happened, then, that Magdalene, blinded by the heartache of seeing that she didn't know how to check Christ's thirst, imagined that the tortured Lamb of God—if He rejected the Falernian wine that pleased the palate and the ambrosia that kindles the imagination—might accept the wine of revenge and rage; perhaps His suffering would be assuaged on tasting the blood of the enemy who had nailed Him to the ignominious cross. With this thought Magdalene approached one of the executioners, the very one who had fastened above Christ's head the mocking inscription of INRI, and, tricking him, she led him far from Calvary, to a deserted spot, and taking advantage of his carelessness, she wounded him in the neck with his own sword, soaked the warm blood in a sponge and returned certain that Jesus would drink. It was this time, on the contrary, when Christ, with superhuman effort, straightened up over His pierced feet and exclaimed with funereal intonation: "I'm thirsty."

Mary Magdalene fell at the foot of the cross, shattered, wringing her hands, and tearing out her loose and long blonde hair by the lock. Her impotence in lessening Christ's thirst was driving her mad, and she began to accuse herself inwardly of her debauched life, feeling on her bowed head the shame and pain of so much dissipation, of the barren, uncultivated land of her conscience where piety found no sanctuary. Many a night, as she flaunted gold on her opulent table and reclined on Tyrian carpets and Persian rugs, the poor, at her door, waited like dogs for scraps from the feast, and honest women, covering their faces with veils, quickened their step to avoid hearing the raucous laughter and lewd songs. For that reason, undoubtedly, now she couldn't enjoy the consolation of quenching Christ's thirst, a thirst that she foolishly believed she could satisfy with the wine of gluttony, the ambrosia of pleasure, or the blood of revenge. On reflection, the sinner's heart softened little by little, and she shed tears of repentance and humility that rose up and flowed out of the corners of her eyes, sliding slowly down her cheeks. Magdalene was weeping so copiously, the tears soaking her clothing and beautiful disheveled hair, that she seemed to lose her spirit. As she lifted her eyes toward Jesus' face, she saw in it an entreaty, a yearning so vivid and so loving that in a fit of inspiration, she cupped her hands and collected those sincere tears of contrition; she then rose and held them up to the Lord's mouth. For the first time, instead of the anguished "I'm thirsty," Jesus responded to Magdalene by parting His lips and drinking eagerly, at the same time that an expression of ineffable happiness transfigured His face.

The story that I've just told has no value with regard to the Church's teachings, nor the least authenticity, nor do I believe that it should be considered anything more than a dream, a fable or a poetic legend discovered amongst the papers of a rabbi who converted to Christianity. Magdalene here isn't the saint: she is only the figure or symbol of the sinner who does not yet know the true path, who still struggles with the noxious aftertaste of sin.

And since the pharisees sought to distort the sense of this apologue, I declare that it only means the following: repentance, humility, and contrition are what most pleases Jesus, and this is a self-evident lesson of the Gospel.*

Blood Bond

If there have been happy marriages, few have been as happy as that of Sabino and Leonarda's. Similar in tastes, age, and financial position, of cheerful disposition and brimming with health, the only thing they lacked—according to others, who are always very busy perfecting somebody else's happiness while causing their own unhappiness—was a child. It should be pointed out that the couple didn't miss having one, wisely thinking that if God didn't bless them with offspring He must have had His reasons. Not once had Leonarda had to wipe away those furtive tears of rage and humiliation that certain reproaches from husbands wring out of wives.

One day Leonarda and Sabino's tranquil life was disturbed by the inopportune visit of Leonarda's only sister, who lived in a distant city under the care of a quite elderly aunt, a lady of strict religious principles. The young woman arrived pale, disfigured, tearful, and sorrowful, and as soon as she rested from her journey, she shut herself in with her sister and brother-in-law, and the consultation lasted a full hour.

Several days later the three of them left together to spend some time at Sabino's country estate, a secluded and very pleasant piece of property. Nobody found this decision strange, because around the end of April said villa is an oasis; and still more explainable seemed the pleasure trip that was undertaken in September by the husband and wife, who did not return from France and England until the following year. What set tongues wagging considerably was that upon coming back they brought with them an adorable baby girl, about whom Leonarda was crazy and to whom she claimed to have given birth in Paris. Since there's never a lack of malicious busybodies, someone thought the infant uncommonly developed for four months, the age attributed to her by her parents. There was gossip, backbiting, finger counting, derisive smiles, and even inquiries and a furious outcry. But time passed, performing its function of applying the balm of beneficial oblivion; Leonarda's sister took refuge in a Carmelite convent; the child grew; the couple evinced more parental love daily; and the rumors, tired of themselves, fell asleep in the arms of indifference.

The truth is that anybody would be proud to have a daughter like Aurora, the name that Leonarda and Sabino gave to their child. Never was there better justification of the preconceptions of ordinary people with respect to children whose births are surrounded by mysterious circumstances, dramas of love and honor. She was possessed of singular beauty, excessively delicate perhaps; intelligence, gentleness, and discretion that amazed everybody; extraordinary talent and exquisite taste; and in addition to all of this, which is concrete and can be expressed with words, there was about her something indefinable—a certain "allure," a charm, a gift for attracting people and enhancing them, for being the center of attention, creating, as Byron said of Haidée,* "an atmosphere of life." Aurora was endowed with all these qualities, and it is no wonder that Sabino and Leonarda literally doted on her.

The girl paid them back in the very same coin. Her filial love had traces of passion, and Aurora usually said that she never intended to marry, not because of not deserting her parents—which would be impossible even to imagine—but to not have to share with anyone the ardent affection that she lavished on them. Those who heard these paradoxes and hyperboles of devotion from such a pink and pretty mouth envied Leonarda and Sabino their appropriated daughter.

Years had passed without Aurora accepting the overtures of any suitor, when one morning there appeared at Sabino's house a gentleman whom we can describe as confident, worldly, and middle-aged, but handsome, well-dressed, and, from all indications, wealthy; he had a very pleasant demeanor and that air of authority peculiar to men who have occupied important positions or attained great triumphs of self-esteem, always living a happy, gratified life. The gentleman asked to speak alone with Sabino and Leonarda, but since they had gone out, he requested permission to see Aurora for a moment. The girl received him in the living room, without becoming agitated, and chatted with him for a time, blushing when the stranger paid her compliments that revealed a deep, keen, secret interest. Their conversation was brief; Aurora's parents returned and the dashing gentleman spoke with them privately. Making a deep bow, his first words were to say that they were looking at a grievous offender—the seducer of Leonarda's sister and Aurora's father—who was prepared to make amends to the extent possible for his errors and misdeeds by recognizing the girl and offering her security, wealth, and a name.

Sabino pondered for a few moments before replying; then he exchanged a meaningful glance with Leonarda, and turning back to the newcomer, said calmly:

"We love Aurora quite a bit more than if she were our own flesh and blood. She's our only charm, the joy of our old age, which is fast approaching, but I assure you that we'll set her free. If she wishes, she can go with you. If she doesn't, promise that she'll stay with us for the rest of her life and that you won't think about claiming her. And so you can see that we won't influence her decision, hide behind those curtains and you'll hear how we question her and what she answers."

The gentleman agreed and hid. Shortly afterwards Aurora walked in, and Sabino put the following questions to her:

"That man who came to talk to us—how did he strike you?"

"Shall I tell the truth, Papa, as always? The whole truth?"

"Yes, of course!"

"Well, I was very taken with him! He struck me as the most . . . most agreeable person . . . I've ever met, Papa."

"That much?"

"Yes, without a doubt. He fascinated me. Aren't you telling me to speak honestly?"

"Would you prefer him to us? Continue being honest."

"It's different from what I feel for you and Mama. I like him . . . in another way."

"Would you be happy living with him?"

"Oh, Papa . . . maybe!"

"Think it over well, my child."

"I don't have to think it over. It's a feeling, and what's really felt isn't thought about. I've never felt this way. I need to ask too: what, has this man . . . asked you for my hand in marriage?"

"Your hand in marriage! Your hand in marriage! It has nothing to do with that!" Leonarda screamed in horror.

"Well ... then? I don't understand," murmured Aurora, distressed.

"Just imagine ... for the sake of argument ... that that man were ... your father! Your real father!"

"My father? I most certainly can't imagine that! I didn't look at him as a father ... nor could I ever! I've already told you that it's different—that I love both of you in another way!"

"Go now, my child," murmured Sabino, confused and dismayed, believing that he heard a plaintive moan behind the curtain. And when Aurora left—obedient, downcast, and silent—the stranger emerged, his face waxen and his eyes crazed.

"I won't bother you any more," he murmured in a husky voice. "I now know what my punishment is. I've tried to study the means of inspiring a certain kind of feeling ... and I inspire it with an ease that has come to fill me with tedium and dread. Midas turned everything into gold; I turn everything into sin. Pure affection, the sacred affection of a father, I'll never be worthy of it. Erase the remembrance of me from Aurora's imagination, and never let her know my name, nor my real identity."

"Perhaps," suggested the sympathetic Leonarda, "the attraction that you exercise over that child, so indifferent toward others, is the blood bond."

"If it is the blood bond, it's a bond that wreaks havoc," replied the libertine, bowing respectfully and leaving, overwhelmed by grief.

The Vision of the Three Magi

The three Magi are returning to their homelands, using a route different than the one by which they came in order to evade the bloodthirsty Herod. It's nighttime; the star no longer guides them, but the moon, shining with a bright and silvery light, illuminates splendidly the desert plain. The dromedaries' shadows are elongated on the smooth, white surface and in the distance resounds the deep roar of a lion.

Balthasar. (Caressing his long, snowy beard and moving his aged head after the manner of one who prophesies.) I don't know what's been happening to me since I knelt in the stable at Bethlehem and paid homage to the Virgin's son, for a prophetic spirit troubles me and I hear the veil that covers the future being drawn back. This tribute of gold that I offered to the Child to recognize him as King, how many, many generations are to render it to him? Tributes he'll receive, not like us, for days, months, and years, but for centuries, tens of centuries, generation after generation, and he'll receive them from the entire Universe, from every race and tongue, from new worlds that will be discovered to acclaim his name. The gold that I presented to him wasn't much: it barely filled the cedar chest in which I brought it. And now I'm imagining that it's been turned into a sea of gold, and I see that for this Child they erect gold temples, chased and wrought gold altars, gold thrones, round which swing white-plumed flabella with gold handles, and that resting on his head is a triple crown, also of solid gold, inlaid with diamonds and precious gems. Waves of gold, flowing from the bowels of the earth, run to the Child's feet; and the strangest thing is that the Child contemplates all of it with a saddened face, and in the end buries his face in his Mother's bosom. Can I have done the wrong thing, oh, savants, in giving him gold? Can it be that the symbol of royal authority doesn't please the celestial infant? I fear that my gift may have been unacceptable and that my offering seemed sacrilegious.

Caspar. (Straightening up on his mount, feeling for his sword, knitting his brows, and speaking with fire in his eyes.) Patriarch of the Magi, my prediction to you was accurate. The newborn King of the Jews is not the ignoble merchant who wishes to hoard countless riches in the cellars of his home. Covetousness degrades the soul and

80

makes it glutinous and ordinary like the clay that, while scorning, we walk on. My gift is the only one that could gratify the Virgin's First-born. You brought him gold because he's a monarch; I brought him myrrh because he's a man. He wanted to be born a man, and calling himself man will be his most valued identity. Myrrh embitters like life, and like life, heals and fortifies; this is what suits the one who shall accomplish manly work, vigorous and salutary work. Do both of you believe that one can be great, noble, and strong without tasting the cup of sorrow? Look at me, oh, savants! I've waged war, I've suffered, I've overcome monsters, I've fought horrible temptation, I've found myself in the hands of my enemies a thousand times, and the breath of martyrdom has grazed my temple. Well, only one day have I cried, and a drop of my tears, falling into the amphora of myrrh, lent it its tonic, agreeable bitterness and perhaps its balsamic scent. I also see the Child, Balthazar, but I see him waging war, routing the enemy, conquering, crushing dragons, subjecting Humanity to his will, suffering, and watering a palm tree with his blood. I did the right thing in bringing him myrrh.

Melchior. (*Timidly, with deep humility.*) I don't know whether I've guessed correctly, but nevertheless, because my heart is overflowing with joy, I presume that the Child is not refusing my gift. You, vener-able and erudite Balthazar, presented him with gold, considering him a king. You, indomitable and valiant Caspar, brought him myrrh, deeming him a man. I, the last of you, the most ignorant, the black-skinned Ethiopian, offered Him grains of frankincense because I had a premonition that He was God.

Balthasar and *Caspar.* (*Astounded.*) God!

Melchior. (*With faith and burning conviction.*) Yes, God. This very minute, in the middle of this peaceful night, I've seen His divinity shine above the clear blue of the heavens where nations are prostrate at His feet and redeemed by Him, and all men made equal by Him. My progeny, the dark race of Ham, no longer differs from the white children of Japheth. The Child's sacred finger has expunged the an-cient curses. You don't recognize Him right at first because this God is different from the gods who are going to die: He neither condemns nor hates nor exterminates; He loves, reconciles, forgives, and just by getting close to Him I perceive an inexplicable serenity in my heart and a glorious peace in my spirit. When I reach my kingdom, I shall open the prisons, discharge the armies, denounce taxes, and free my concubines; and I will appear unarmed in the middle of the public square to confess my mistakes and to allow my enemies, if they wish, to take revenge on me.

Balthasar. You confuse me, Melchior. Your belief seems like lunacy.

Caspar. I don't understand you fully, Melchior. Your belief strikes me as effeminate, unbecoming a king.

Melchior. I can't defend it rationally. I act on what I feel.

Balthasar. My gift was exquisite.

Caspar. Mine was worthy and noble.

Melchior. Mine expresses my unimportance, and only signifies adoration.

Balthasar. By combining all three in one, perhaps we would come by something that made the prodigious Child smile.

Caspar. It's not possible. Where can there be a gift simultaneously befitting the King, the Man, and the God?

The moon shines with a softer brightness, more mysteriously gentle and dreamlike. The desert looks like a lake of silver. Silhouetted against the horizon is the figure of a woman splendidly adorned and richly dressed—a beautiful, tearful woman with long blonde hair that falls to the hem of her gown. In her hands she carries a myrrhic goblet full of nard ointment, whose fragrance spreads and impregnates the clothing of the Magi, and even goes to their heads like a delicate, penetrating mist of perfume. And the three Magi, dismounting and kneeling on the desert sand, envy, with saintly envy, the gift of Magdalene the sinner.

A Galician Mother*

It was the time in which the vipers of discord, regaled in the bloody bosom of the civil war,* stirred in every town, maybe in every home. Black rancor, violent hatred, and blazing fury, assuming bodily form in those horrible snakes, weakened family ties, separated brother from brother, and sowed fratricidal instincts in their souls. Today it is difficult for us to comprehend the virulent hostility of that period, and perhaps when history, in a serious, calm voice, describes scenes of such tragic days, we accuse it of overstating the case, without realizing that the greatest tragedies are precisely the ones that usually remain hidden.

Nevertheless, in some Spanish provinces, political passions were calmer and more subdued, and one of them was the garden of Galicia, site of the pleasant and charming city of Pontevedra. Luis María was born and grew up there, and then studied theology and ethics at the seminary in Orense to become ordained. He was the only child of poor parents. His father, from Aragón, was a traveling salesman who sold blankets and silk handkerchiefs; his mother, a villager, was born near Poyo, in the vicinity of the lovely Helenes and was such a plain woman that she didn't know how to read or even sew because she earned a living with a distaff and a shapeless and primitive homemade loom if there ever was one. Luis María turned out to be studious, devout, gentle, dependable, a great helper at Mass and candlesnuffer, and announced at a very early age that he dreamed of being a priest. His mother pressed his father to appeal to a certain wealthy and charitable Aragonese gentleman, Don Ramón de Bolea, for money to pay for the boy's studies. The request was so well-received that not only did Don Ramón pay for his education, he also sponsored him when he was ordained, and shortly afterwards, with the new priest's father dead, the generous patron summoned the young man to be his chaplain. Luis María held the post for two years, much to the pleasure of his benefactor, but when the local parish became available, and was to be filled by His Excellency, Don Ramón de Bolea himself sought and obtained it for his protégé, because the bishop of Teruel refused the powerful gentleman nothing.

On seeing himself entrusted with the care of souls, holder of what could properly be called a "position," Luis María remembered, above all else, his mother, who was vegetating all alone back in the village, swingling, spinning, and weaving yarn. He made the trip, a long and arduous one at the time, and didn't return to his parish without the little old woman, who out of humility and abnegation began by refusing to accompany him. It was necessary for the son to convince his mother how much he needed her to run the house and prepare meals and to prevent gossip if he engaged a young female domestic. Finally the old woman consented and went with her son, bursting with pride and joy in the bottom of her heart.

They settled in the town, eager to live quietly and huddled together, like birds in their humble nest. When civil conflicts began to flare up, Luis María made a studied effort to remove and distance himself from them. The scenes of cruelty and barbarity filled him with terror and revulsion, as did the beatings of Christinists and Carlists, the shameless and insulting verses that the young women of opposing sides yelled at each other from rooftop to rooftop, the news of clashes in which so many unfortunate men died, and the throat cuttings of clergy that had bloodied the steps of the altar itself. The parish priest sensed that not even through class allegiance could he overcome his repugnance at such savagery and atrocity. He had taken after his mother: timid, meek, indifferent to politics, accessible only to piety and tenderness; Galician, not Aragonese; a Christian, but not a Carlist. "Blessed are the peacemakers," he would repeat sadly when he heard a frightful piece of news—the burning of a village, the sacrifice of a few prisoners executed with harquebuses in reprisals.

It's characteristic of such anxious and feverish times that nobody, for as much as he wants to, can take a neutral stance. In the town, among the most divided and bellicose in all of Aragón, they wouldn't allow the priest not to have an opinion. Two circumstances caused public speculation to place Luis María in the

camp of the Pretender's supporters: first, that he fervently fulfilled his priestly duties, that he was chaste, austere, cautious in
speech and timid in action; the second, being the favorite, protégé, chaplain, creature, in short, of that Don Ramón de Bolea,
formerly the most influential man in the town, today leader of a
rebel band. The Aragonese people, simple and logical, who asso-
ciate gratitude with support, reckoned Luis María, therefore,
among the "Serviles," but not among the declared and open
ones, rather among the furtive and shamefaced, who were infinitely more loathed. The many brave Christinists that the town
sheltered looked askance at the priest; they suspected him of
collusion and of passing secret information and making accusations to Don Ramón de Bolea, whose troops patrolled just a few
leagues away, eager to settle a score with the "Nationals."

Luis María felt the hostility in the atmosphere, and he flinched
and withdrew more and more, because he was of the sort who
do not fight, not even in self-defense. His mystic ardor, already
intense, increased, and the more ascetic and haggard his enemies
saw him, the more they believed him committed to conspiring
for the triumph of Absolutism and its servile supporters. The
town's hatred began to result in deeds: every time the priest's
mother went out to shop, Aragonese peasant women reviled her
and called her rebel at the top of their voices, and in front of
their windows groups congregated shouting patriotic songs. One
holiday afternoon, as the young men came back strumming gui-
tars and singing songs with cutting allusions, some daring soul
hurled a stone that shattered a window pane of the rectory. The
mother cried softly on closing the shutters, while Luis María,
kneeling in front of the statue of Our Lady, prayed without moving, turning a deaf ear to the crash of the thrown rocks, which
continued smashing the windows to pieces.

A few days afterwards tremendous news spread throughout
the town that Bolea had caught two local men, impassioned Nationals accused of giving beatings to Serviles, and had executed
them against a wall with harquebuses. On returning from the
market the next day, the priest's mother, intimidated and apprehensive, heard as she went by, no longer abuse, taunts and scorn,
but ominous threats, warnings that sent chills up the spine.
Trembling, the shaken woman locked herself inside the house,

where she found Luis María in prayer, asking God to forgive his patron Bolea the blood he had spilled.

Pallid, silent, downcast, and hiding their feelings, mother and son ate supper; and when they were getting ready to go to bed a tremendous din arose in the street, and loud knocks on the door were heard. The mother hurried to ask, without opening up, what was going on, and a gruff, mocking voice answered:

"Let the priest show himself and we'll tell him the name of a parishioner who's dying and wants to make his confession."

Luis María's hearing this and rushing to the window happened all at once. But his mother, perhaps for the first time in her life, intervened firmly and stopped him, grabbing him by the wrist with unwonted stamina, with all her peasant-woman strength, increased a hundredfold by anguish, and turning him brusquely aside, clutched the window latch.

"Don't look," she ordered in an imperious tone, a tone different from the mild, affectionate one with which she always spoke to her son. "Move away. Stand back. *I'll* look, don't you worry."

Before Luis María could object, she blew out the oil lamp in one puff to avoid being recognized, opened the window impetuously, and leaned out.

The barbarian, who already had his shotgun aimed, fired, and the mother, her chest riddled, toppled over toward the inside, into the arms of the son for whom she was accepting death.

Soft-Boiled Eggs

The family of Don Donato López resembled other bourgeois families that enjoy public esteem and respect the law and the foundations on which society, like an iron tower in the midst of bamboo poles, is upheld.

López figured among the people with sound ideas, and he tolerated neither divisive doctrines nor impiety in religious matters. Mrs. López and their daughters frequented churches, were accustomed to making financial offerings and, since they believed sincerely, sincerely condemned unbelievers. For their father the girls professed a sacred respect, persuaded that rectitude and morality inspired his teachings and his actions, and that he was the model of an honest citizen and a good man. When practicing their faith, they were certain of following the impulse of a Christian head of family. Upon their return from hearing a sermon or Mass, from visiting the poor or from sharing chores with other members of Roperito, López's girls gathered happily about their papa, who, after questioning and approving, caressed them and joked around with them, while feeling, deep inside, very kind and very perfect.

Don Donato usually had two soft-boiled eggs for breakfast, and he always demanded that they be done to a turn: not so overcooked that they were hard, nor so undercooked that the white wouldn't stick, partially solidified and soft, to the shell. The cook had this difficult balancing act down to an art, and Don Donato savored contentedly his frugal, wholesome breakfast.

But it so happened that the cook was dismissed for some extraordinary pilfering, and the soft-boiled eggs began to arrive now hard, now runny, never as Mr. López liked them. On seeing her father annoyed and refusing breakfast, Enriqueta, the eldest of his daughters, bought a small appliance of the sort called "infernos," that are fueled with alcohol, and bringing the water to a boil, she got ready to cook the eggs herself, on the dining room table, not without asking López how she ought to proceed to achieve the desired result.

"You have to say the Apostles' Creed three times," replied the father, "and when you finish saying them the eggs are cooked to perfection, just right."

The girls laughed at the recipe, and the eldest exclaimed:

"Well, start praying, Papa, while I look after putting the eggs in and removing them at the right time. Let's see!"

Don Donato López, who was also laughing, began the task of reciting the prayer to continue the joke: "I believe in God the Father Almighty, Creator of heaven and earth; in Jesus Christ, His only Son . . ."

At this juncture, the same as if the moment of garroting him had arrived, Don Donato was unable to go on: he didn't remember another word; he broke out in an anguished sweat. The phrases of the forgotten Creed, even though they seemed to awaken and stir, scattered about in the recesses of his memory, did not come to his rescue. He felt himself turning red, very red, while Enriqueta, who had stopped laughing, was staring at him and growing pale, unsuccessful in holding onto the handle of the saucepan to prevent the boiling water from spilling out.

And because young children lack judgment, Laurita, the chubby nine-year-old, burst out laughing and shouted:

"Mama! Mama! Come here! Oh, what a joke! Papa doesn't know the Creed!"

The Torn Lace

The wedding ceremony of Micaelita Aránguiz and Bernardo de Meneses was scheduled for 10 P.M. at the home of the bride. I had been invited but was unable to attend, and so I was very surprised to learn the following day that Micaelita, at the foot of the very altar, let out a clear and resounding No when the Bishop of San Juan de Arce asked her if she took Bernardo as her husband. The Bishop, taken aback, repeated the question, which Micaelita again answered in the negative; and Bernardo, after facing for a quarter of an hour the most ridiculous predicament imaginable, had no choice but to withdraw, which at one stroke dispersed the guests and put an end to their union.

Such cases are not unheard of, and we usually read about them in the newspapers, but they occur among the unassuming, among people of very modest means, in circles where social conventions do not prevent the frank and spontaneous expression of feeling and choice.

The peculiar aspect of the scene caused by Micaelita was the milieu in which it unfolded. I had the impression of being able to picture the setting, and I was disconsolate at not having contemplated it with my own eyes. I imagined the crowded drawing room, the select gathering, the women dressed in silk and velvet with necklaces of precious stones, carrying white mantillas to cover their heads during the ceremony; the men with their glittering decorations or displaying the insignia of military orders on the front of their dress coats; the bride's mother, richly attired, very busy and solicitous, going from group to group, receiving congratulations; the bride's little sisters, emotional and very prettily dressed, the older one in pink, the younger one in blue, both proudly wearing turquoise bracelets, a gift from their future brother-in-law; the Bishop who is to join them in marriage, alternately serious and affable, smiling, tossing off urbane jokes or discreet praise, while in the background there is a sense of mystery in the chapel that is filled with flowers, a deluge of white roses that go from the floor to the little dome, where spokes of snow-white roses and lilacs converge, artistically arranged on green branches; and on the altar, the effigy of the Virgin, patroness of the aristocratic mansion, half-hidden by a curtain of orange blossoms, the contents of a section of a railway car full of orange blossoms that were sent from Valencia by the bride's uncle and godfather, a very wealthy landowner, who did not come in person because of old age and infirmity; details that are exchanged by word of mouth—estimating the magnificent inheritance that Micaelita will receive, another source of happiness for the married couple who will go to Valencia to spend their honeymoon. In a group of men I imagined the groom, somewhat nervous, slightly pale, nibbling involuntarily at his mustache, lowering his head to respond to the subtle jokes and flattering comments directed to him.

And, finally, I saw a kind of apparition appear at the entryway of the door that opens on the interior rooms—the bride, whose features are barely perceived under the delicate tulle veil, and who passes by with her silk gown rustling while the diamond heirloom of the nuptial adornment in her hair shines like a field of dew . . . And now the ceremony begins, the pair go forward accompanied by the bride's father and the groom's mother, the white figure kneels by the side of the slender and graceful one of her fiancé . . . Members of the family crowd together in the foreground, friends and onlookers search for a good place to see, and in the midst of the silence and respectful attention of the spectators . . . the Bishop formulates a question, which is answered with a *No* as sharp as an explosion, as emphatic as gunfire. And, still imagining the scene, I pictured the movement of the groom, who turns around, pained; the forward motion of the bride's mother who rushes forth as if to defend and protect her daughter, the insistence of the Bishop—a manifestation of his surprise, the shudder of the crowd, the suspense produced by the questions that spread instantly: "What's happening? What is it? The bride has become ill? She says *No*? Impossible . . . But is it true? What a turn of events!"

Within the context of social life all of this constitutes a terrible drama. And in Micaelita's case it was a riddle as well as a drama. The reason for the sudden refusal was never learned for certain.

Micaelita would say only that she had changed her mind and that she was her own person, free to turn back, even if it was at the foot of the altar, as long as she had not pronounced the "I do." Close friends of the family racked their brains, expressing improbable suppositions. Beyond question was what everybody observed until the fateful moment—that bride and groom were content and very loving with each other; and the girl friends who went in to admire the bride dressed in her finery, minutes before the scandal, reported that she was deliriously happy, and so full of dreams and contentment that she would not change places with anybody. These were details that served to obscure further the strange enigma that for a long time was food for gossips who were irritated by the mystery and willing to explain it in an unfavorable light.

Three years later, when almost nobody remembered any longer the incident at Micaelita's wedding, I ran into her at a fashionable spa, where her mother had come to bathe in the mineral water. Nothing facilitates an acquaintance like life at a bathing resort, and Miss Aránguiz became such a close friend of mine that one afternoon, as we were walking toward the church, she revealed her secret to me, stating that she was giving me permission to divulge it, because she was certain that nobody would believe such a simple explanation.

"It was the silliest thing. So silly that I refused to say what it was. People always attribute events to profound and far-reaching causes without noticing that at times our fate is determined by trifles, the most insignificant trivialities ... But they're trivialities that mean something, and for certain people they mean too much. You'll see what happened. And I don't understand why no one noticed it because the incident occurred right there, in front of everybody, but they didn't take heed because it really was a matter of an instant.

"You already know that my marriage to Bernardo de Meneses seemed to bring together all the conditions and guarantees that make for happiness. Besides, I admit that my fiancé appealed to me a great deal, more than any of the men I knew then and know now; I think I was in love with him. The only thing I regretted was not being able to scrutinize his character. Some people found him foul-tempered, but I always saw him as courteous and considerate, as gentle as a lamb, and I feared that he was adopting a façade intended to deceive me and to conceal a cruel and harsh disposition. A thousand times I cursed the subordinate position of the single woman, for whom it is an impossibility to keep an eye on her fiancé, and to probe reality and obtain honest and reliable information, the only kind that would set my mind at ease, even if it hurt. I tried subjecting Bernardo to several tests, and he came through them fine. His conduct was so proper that I came to believe that I could trust my future and happiness to him without any fear.

"The day of the wedding arrived. In spite of my natural emotion, on getting dressed in my white gown I noticed once again the magnificent lace ruffle that adorned it, a gift from my fiancé. That old piece of genuine Alençon lace had belonged to his family; it was a third of a yard wide—a marvel—of an exquisite design, perfectly preserved, and worthy of a museum showcase. Bernardo had given it to me as a gift, extolling its value, which irritated me, because for as much as the lace was worth, my future husband should have assumed that it meant little to me.

"At that solemn moment, on seeing the lace set off by the rich satin of my dress, it seemed to me that the extremely delicate needlework signified a promise of happiness, and that its texture so fragile and at the same time so strong held two hearts captive in its dainty meshes. I was fascinated by this fancy when I began to walk toward the drawing room where my fiancé awaited me at the door. On rushing forward to greet him full of joy, for the last time before belonging to him in body and soul, the lace got caught on a piece of the ironwork on the door, with such bad luck that on trying to free myself I heard the peculiar noise of a sizable tear, and I could see that a strip of the magnificent adornment hung over the lower part of my gown. But I also saw something else: Bernardo's face, distorted and disfigured by the most intense anger; his eyes blazing, his mouth half-open, ready to utter reproaches and abuse . . . He didn't go that far because he was surrounded by people, but in that fleeting instant a curtain was raised and a soul was laid bare.

"I must have turned pale. Fortunately the tulle of my veil covered my face. Inside, something was cracking and breaking into pieces, and the elation with which I had crossed the threshold of the drawing room changed into profound horror. It was as if I had always seen Bernardo with that expression of wrath, harshness and contempt that I had just discovered in his face. This conviction took hold of me, and with it came another one: the conviction that I couldn't, that I wouldn't give myself to such a man, not then, not ever . . . And, nevertheless, I continued approaching the altar, I knelt, I listened to the Bishop's exhortations . . . But when I was asked, the truth—impetuous and terrible—sprang to my lips . . .

"That No was bursting out without my intending it to. I was saying it to myself . . . for everyone to hear!"

"And why didn't you state the real reason when so many comments were made?"

"I repeat: because of its very simplicity. They never would have understood. I preferred to allow people to believe that there were reasons of the kind that are called serious."

Logic

Justino Guijarro is worthy of mention in the annals of the personal history that laymen call fictional literature. Even though the drama of his life hasn't gained the fame that it deserves, as a significant and curious instance, those of us who met him and heard his last confession at a terrible time should not allow the memory of such an extraordinary man to be consigned to oblivion.

First of all, let future generations know that Justino Guijarro died on the scaffold. Don't go assuming (let's say at the outset) that Justino was, in the world of the living, a professional criminal, a leader of a band of robbers. Don't go confusing him either with those who break into houses to loot them or those who kill people on the spot to make off with a billfold full of banknotes. Even less should he be likened to those fanatics possessed of a brutal instinct who strangle a woman on account of jealousy or because she scorned them. Justino was never ruled by raging concupiscence or contemptible greed inasmuch as he lived a life devoted to study and meditation, immersed and absorbed in the unfathomable depths of thought, subjecting ideas to the scrutiny of a microscope, ideas that other less finicky thinkers accept without question. Justino stood out moreover for his vehement religiosity, and think what he may about it, the reader will have to recognize that an eloquent demonstration of it is what he's going to learn by perusing these pages, where I disclose the secret of an exceptional human being, unique perhaps.

Justino was born with a narrow, sharp-pointed skull, an exterior sign of the lofty nature of his meditations and the spiritual aspect of his way of life. From childhood he reasoned so precisely and soundly that his ratiocinations were like wedges driven in the brain. He pursued the deductions of a premise to their ultimate conclusions, and woe to the one who conceded the least point to him in a discussion; a slight concession furnished

Guijarro irrefutable arguments with which to wear down his opponent and vanquish him in the end. He was feared; nobody wanted to challenge him, and people said that he embodied the spirit of the scholastics of the Middle Ages who were so accomplished in persuasive discourse.

With the same method that he applied to intellectual questions, Justino solved the problems of his practical life. This was a doubly ticklish undertaking because everybody realizes that this miserable life that we endure—without being able to avoid it—is complex, roundabout and contradictory at times, as only it can be, and that the most inflexible and obstinate of thinkers finds himself forced, if not into stumbling seven times a day, then at least into reaching an accommodation with circumstances ten times as often. Justino, however, was ignorant of compromises and chose to undergo seventy daily clashes and be taken just as many more times for being foolish and insufferable. The world is such that it doesn't conceive of anybody not following the straight path, even if it leads to disaster.

The annoyances that Justino experienced must have contributed in no small measure to firing his fertile imagination and suggesting to him the peculiar solutions that will soon be described.

Justino was married; his religious logic had inclined him toward matrimony from the earliest days of his youth. He went many years without offspring, but finally there appeared unmistakable signs in his wife that a blessed event was drawing near, and a strong, robust, and lovely baby boy was born, the kind of child that makes parents swell with pride.

Nevertheless, Justino, instead of delighting and rejoicing in his fatherhood, took to turning depressed and melancholy. Every time they brought him the child, whom the mother, filled with enthusiasm, held up to be kissed by his father, Justino's face became taut, and his eyes, clouded from meditation, emitted a sad, sorrowful glimmer.

"On seeing my son (I'm transcribing verbatim here the words of the illustrious, unknown thinker whose story I'm telling), I couldn't feel what your common father feels—a puerile and merely instinctive joy, an animal impulse . . . On the contrary, a host of oppressive and confusing thoughts weighed on my mind.

The responsibility that burdened me was immense and incalculable; the future of a man, of a rational being rested in my hands, in my care. When I speak of *future*, you'll understand, knowing me as you do from my confession, that I don't refer to the future as other parents understand it, a period that only comprises the days of a fleeting existence. Money, honors, position, health . . . What do these ephemeral riches mean to someone who observes—with intelligence, with reason, with, in short, superior powers—the immense march of centuries slowly unfolding, and who considers, in the midst of the spasms of a sublime vertigo, the infinite horizon of eternity?

"My son's body, a mass of pink and white flesh, didn't exist for me, or if it existed, it had no value whatsoever. But his soul, his immortal soul—a divine flash transmitted to matter! 'Save his soul,' I was told continuously by the crystalline voice of Logic, my teacher and infallible adviser. 'Save his soul, spare him from sin, open wide for him the golden gates of heaven.' And to save his soul, I had but one recourse, and, after a long struggle with myself, I set it in motion. One night, while his mother was asleep exhausted from the breast-feeding, I approached my son's cradle and threw the sheet fold over his tiny face, then the two pillows; I pressed the palms of my hands with all my strength . . . and I kept pressing like that until . . . until I saved him, sending him off to enjoy eternal happiness.

"My son's death," Justino continued after a profound pause, "was attributed to natural causes. But I now confronted a problem that was no less grave—that of my own salvation. Logic told me that, if I saved another person, for significant reasons I was in a position to save myself, since salvation is the supreme end to which our passage on earth should be directed. On saving my son, I had burdened my conscience, without being able to avoid it, with a sin. It was imperative to atone for it. All this was logical, and even more logical that if death took me by surprise, ill-prepared, the business of my soul—the only important business—was failing.

"I needed, therefore, two things: to do penance in this life and to know the exact moment of my death, in order to be prepared and ready. Suicide was out of the question—the person who commits suicide doesn't die in a state of grace. It was necessary to conceive of another combination, and logically I came up with a brilliant one. I waited for the time when my wife, heartbroken since the baby's passing, was returning from church, where she had gone to confession and received communion, and taking advantage of her spiritual preparedness and the moment in which she bent down to unlace her boots, I lunged at her armed with a kitchen knife, and in the first thrust . . . I saved her. When she died, I turned myself in, covered with blood, to the police. My parricide (as they termed it) was, according to them, patent and horrible. I was sentenced to death, and during the long days spent in prison I had time for self-mortification, for reconciling myself with God (I hope), and for arranging all my matters of conscience in such a way, that on offering my neck to the expiatory iron collar,* the chances of my saving myself too will logically be ninety-nine out of a hundred.

"The only thing that confuses me, the only thing that has troubled my spirit, almost absorbed already in contemplation of the extraterrestrial, is that the priest who comes to console me in this chapel, instead of praising the logic of my conduct, seems convinced that I did nothing except commit atrocities. It's true that he's a poor, ignorant priest, and I fear that for lack of education and philosophical training he doesn't understand the sublimity of my conception, the admirable equilibrium of my acts. In vain I repeat to him over and over again an irrefutable argument. Killing my wife and child was a sin; I recognize it and deplore it. But if all of us are sinners and I couldn't boast of having lived without sinning, at least my sins are of such a nature that they've opened up paradise to the two beings I loved most, and my expiation will probably open it up for me. When I set forth this incisive conclusion to the priest, a slow-witted, simple man, his only response is to shake his head and murmur certain phrases that I consider illogical on all accounts, for example: 'God's mercy extends to the wicked, and more understandably to dreamers and maniacs and lunatics. Forget about logic and pray and weep and repent as much as you can.'"

The Substitute

There isn't anybody who hasn't found himself in the difficult situation of having to give, very gingerly and in the least painful manner, a piece of bad news. I was entrusted for the first time with this unpleasant task when Don Ambrosio Corchado's only sister, Lasmarcas's widow, died suddenly.

I wasn't acquainted with Don Ambrosio, but I was, on the other hand, one of three or four of the deceased Lasmarcas's faithful friends, and visited his widow frequently, always receiving a warm, open welcome. On winter evenings we took refuge in her small sitting room where she kept a well-stoked brazier and where the double curtains and thick shutters blocked out drafts of air and the noise of rain. With each one settled in his seat and place of preference, we would chat animatedly until teatime, a simple, attractively served snack which included cookies and buns that, perhaps for economical reasons, she herself baked.

The homemade tea tasted heavenly to us and we ended our soirées satisfied and relaxed because Lasmarcas's widow was a woman with a very pleasant manner—neither timid nor meddlesome, neither extremely malicious nor foolishly naive; and as a friend, dependable and loyal, as I wish all men were. Upon learning that she had been found dead in her bed, struck down by a serous effusion, we felt the biting cold of "the great beyond," the shudder caused by a sudden blast of frigid air that whips us in the face on entering a pantheon. Just like that do we go! Just like that do our lives disappear in a breath, lives seemingly so active and full of plans, hopes, and longstanding interests! We had just gone to her home the previous night for our get-together; it seemed that we could still see her offering us a portion of bread pudding, which she praised, assuring us that it was a recipe given to her by the nuns of the Annunciation order.

When we, her close friends, were informed of her demise, it was decided that I would undertake to notify her brother. Don

Ambrosio Corchado lived about six miles away from the city where his sister lived, on a piece of property that he never left, and where the widow spent her summers. Wealthy and not very sociable, Don Ambrosio typified the confirmed bachelor: he didn't want to disturb the world and was even less tolerant of the world disturbing him. In his own way he got along very well, making improvements on his country estate, directing the farm work, and feeding chickens and pigs. That was all we knew about Don Ambrosio. To carry out my mission without delay, I ordered a carriage, and forty-five minutes later it arrived at my door, with ringing of bells and clatter of squeaky wheels.

I got in the ramshackle vehicle and we started off in the direction of the estate. It was a splendid morning—vibrant, cheerful, sunny, and bright, serving as a prelude to the spring that was approaching. Settled in the rear of the surrey, looking out the window and watching the picturesque countryside roll by, I was overcome, in spite of the nice weather and pure, clean air, by a painful melancholy, a kind of apprehension and awkward timidity.

My heart sank thinking about what I should tell Don Ambrosio and how I would begin to make him understand in a way that would soften the blow. I clearly imagined the dramatic impact of the moment. Don Ambrosio had no other sister, nor any other family in the world. Mrs. Lasmarcas was not survived by children whom he could take in and who would gladden his solitary old age. A sister! The person who is our companion from the time of the cradle, with whom we've played as children, whose blood flows in our veins, who has shared our first innocent pleasures, our first tantrums; who has been our confidante, who covered up for us, who witnessed our pranks, and was moved by our first adolescent infatuations; the little mother, the natural friend, the unselfish accomplice, the defender. The person who knows no other attachment, whose only surviving family member is a sister, what will he feel on learning that he's lost her? Undoubtedly, what the tree feels when an axe is driven in the middle of its trunk, when it is cloven and cut apart. Besides, her death was so sudden! Perhaps Don Ambrosio had even built up his hopes, time and time again, that his sister, younger than he, would be at his side in his last hour.

These thoughts excited my imagination and caused such undefinable anguish that when the carriage stopped in front of the main entrance to the estate my eyes were moist with tears. I brought my emotion under control and jumped out. Seeing a man who was leveling off the sand in the courtyard, I inquired about Don Ambrosio, and he very willingly dropped his hoe and guided me, going through a fruit orchard and beautiful gardens adorned with fountains, to a meadowland where several farm hands worked at mowing grass and piling it on carts, under the watchful eye of a little old man in a straw hat wearing spectacles with blue lenses. It was Don Ambrosio in person.

He greeted me with surprise, and when I told him that I was there on a matter of some importance, he was quite gracious. He explained to me that that little meadow produced annually more than thirty cartloads of dry grass that sold like hotcakes, and yielding to his propensity to discuss only what touched on matters of a practical nature, he added that he was afraid it was going to rain and that he was hastening the harvest in the hope of gathering the grass in good condition. Afterwards he pointed out to me a corner of the meadow were a limpid brook flowed and asked me if I thought the current of the water was sufficient to drive a flour mill that he intended to construct there. His wrinkled little face and hollow voice turned serious when explaining his plans. In the meantime, I was seeking a way to break the bad news, but two or three hints about the widow's poor health elicited no more than a distracted, "Is that so, is that so." It was then that I decided to press harder and went to the heart of the matter: my real reason for being there was that his sister, somewhat ill since yesterday . . .

"Yes, winter discomforts, annoying colds," he replied absentmindedly.

His reaction upset me and I let out the two words "grave illness." Through his blue lenses I saw that the old man was blinking.

"Grave? And the doctor, what does he say?"

"There wasn't time to consult him," I exclaimed. "You know how it is, these sudden things . . ."

"Well, consult him, consult him," he repeated, turning around to watch a cart go by loaded to the hilt. "Hey," he shouted to the farm hands, "you idiots, half of the grass is falling off on you! Secure the load well, good Lord!"

"Didn't I tell you," I interrupted him, raising my voice too, "that there was no time for consultation? It was sudden . . . her . . ." I was choking on the terrible word, but I finally got it out: "Her . . . her death!"

Don Ambrosio took a step backward. His blue lenses sparkled in the sun. Stammering, he said:

"In other words . . . in . . ."

". . . other words, your sister, yes, was found dead this morning . . . in bed . . . a serous effusion."

The old man kept quiet, swinging his head. After a pause, he cleared his throat and said calmly:

"Bless her soul! The poor thing's time was up. Well, if you need anything for the funeral, of course . . . you know you can rely on me. Even if it costs a little more . . . do you understand? Everything should be done with dignity. Don't be put off by, give or take, a hundred *duros*."

"You won't be attending the funeral?" I asked, devouring the old man with my eyes.

"Well, look. With the meadow only half mowed and the weather just right to do it . . . impossible. Things would be in fine shape if I weren't here to keep an eye out! And it just so happens that tomorrow the builder's coming to discuss details of the mill. You have to scrutinize the contract or these people will take you to the cleaners. And what's your opinion? Will the current be strong enough? Right now, in springtime, there's no problem, but in the fall?"

I left there in such a state of exasperation that I slammed the carriage door upon closing it, furthering the ruin of the decrepit surrey. Once more I was in the grip of an insurmountable sadness; I felt ridiculous, and the wretchedness of our nature overwhelmed me as I thought about that little old man, who was as insensitive as a stone, and whose only concern was his meadow and mill, who forgot about the proximity of death. A fine bit of foolishness—my precautions, my apprehension in conveying the news! Suddenly a singular idea occurred to me. My fit of sensitivity compensated for Don Ambrosio's indifference. The dead woman's real "brother" was me—I was the one who had felt the brotherly pain, I, who had substituted myself, willingly and sorrowfully, for the flesh-and-blood brother. In the moral world as in the physical nothing is lost, and all those who have a right to a certain sum of affection collect it, if not from the one who owes it to them, then from another generous payer. Consoled by these thoughts, I stuck my head out the window and said to the coachman (I really did say it):

"Faster. I need to make arrangements for my sister's funeral."

From the Beyond

Don Javier de Campuzano was nearing death and saw it coming without fear; having repented for his sins, he trusted in the mercy of the One who died because His extended to all of mankind. Only one concern troubled him some nights, those when insomnia plague the elderly. He wondered if, after he was dead, dissension, nasty fights, and lawsuits over property would arise between his two children and sole heirs. Don Javier was a very affluent landowner, a very wealthy man, and he was not unaware that the most contested struggles over money are always started by the rich. Certain extremely bitter memories from his youth contributed to increasing his apprehension. He remembered having been in litigation for a long time with his older brother; it was a complicated, fierce, and interminable lawsuit that began by cooling off their fraternal affection and ended up transforming it into bloody hatred. The sin of wishing his brother all sorts of misfortune, of having reviled and slandered him, and even— dreadful memory!—of having waited for him one night in the shadows of an oak grove for the purpose of challenging him to a terrible fight, was the burden that Don Javier had on his conscience for many years. In intention he had been fratricidal, and he trembled on imagining that his children, whom he loved dearly, might come to detest each other because of a handful of money.

Nature had given Don Javier an eloquent example and a harsh lesson: his two children, a son and a daughter, were twins. On joining them from their beginnings in the same womb, on bringing them into the world at the same time, God had imperiously commanded them to love each other. With his imagination affected since their birth, Don Javier reflected only that two beings with identical bloodline, conceived at the very same moment in a woman's womb, could, nevertheless, abhor each other to the point of violence. To prevent jealousy of paternal affection from

103

breeding hatred, Don Javier provided his son with a military career and almost always kept him away from home. Only when he recognized that old age and ailments were pushing him to the grave did he summon José María and permit his filial solicitude to alternate with María Josefa's. By dint of reflection, the old man had devised a plan, and he began to implement it by calling his daughter aside, in great secrecy, and saying to her solemnly:

"My dear daughter, before your brother arrives I have to inform you of something that is important to you. Listen to me carefully and don't forget a single one of my words. I don't need to affirm that I love you a great deal, but moreover, your sex should be shielded in a special way and receive greater protection. I've thought about improving your lot without anybody being able to dispute what I'm giving you. As soon as I end my days . . . as soon as you pray for me a little . . . go to the farmhouse at Guadeluz, and in the large room downstairs, where that very old heavy chest is, the one that's supposed to be Gothic, count from your left, starting at the door, sixteen tiles—pay close attention—sixteen, the number of ounces in a pound, do you understand? Lift the seventeenth one, that has a kind of sign of a cross, and a few others around it. Under the tiles you'll see a stone, secured with strong mortar, and a large iron ring. Remove the mortar, dislodge the stone, and a hiding place will appear. In it you'll find one million *reales** in gold coins. It's my savings of many years! The one million is yours, yours alone; I'm leaving it to you with no strings attached. Now, keep this to yourself and let's not say another word about the matter. When I'm gone . . ."

María Josefa smiled sweetly, expressed her gratitude in tender words, and assured him that she wished she would never have occasion to collect the substantial bequest. José María arrived that very night, and the two siblings, relieving each other by turns, kept a bedside vigil over Don Javier, who was failing visibly. His last moments, his last hour, were not long in coming, and in the middle of the muscular contractions of painful throes, María Josefa noticed that her dying father was squeezing her hand in an expressive manner, and she thought that his eyes, already glassy, devoid of inner light, were clearly saying to hers:

"Remember, sixteen tiles ... one million *reales* in gold coins ..."

The first few days after the funeral were devoted, naturally, to sorrow and tears, to expressions of condolence and an outpouring of grief. Brother and sister, depressed, their eyelids red, said very little to each other, and nothing that had anything to do with mundane affairs. However, it became necessary to open the will and to confer with notaries, attorneys, and executors, and one night when José María and María Josefa were alone in the huge drawing room and the faint light of the oil lamp brightened the darkness as it died out, the sister approached her brother, touched him on the shoulder, and spoke timidly, in a very soft voice:

"José María, I must tell you something ... something strange ... about Papa."

"Tell me, love. Something strange?"

"Yes, you'll see. And you'll be astonished. There are one million *reales* in gold coins, hidden in the farmhouse at Guadeluz."

"No, silly," exclaimed José María with unexpected passion, taken by surprise. "You didn't understand it right. By no means. Where all that money is hidden is at the Corchada pastureland."

"For heaven's sake, Joselillo! I'm telling you that Papa explained it to me very clearly, in great detail. In the large room downstairs you have to count sixteen tiles on the left, from the door, and at the seventeenth is the stone with the large iron ring that conceals the treasure."

"I assure you that you're mistaken. Papa gave me so many particulars that there's no doubt. At the pastureland, beside the old abandoned sheepfold wall, there's a kind of trough where the livestock used to drink. At the back is a small, half-ruined trunk, and at the foot of it a flagstone broken around the corner. By freeing that flagstone you find a tile niche, and in it one million in gold coins."

"My dear brother, I tell you that's impossible! Believe me. When Papa sent for you he was already going downhill, very close to breathing his last. Maybe his mind wasn't sound, poor thing. I have his words etched right here ..."

"María," José declared, taking her hand after meditating for a moment, "the fact is that there are two depositories. It's the only way to make sense out of what we're telling each other. Papa advised me that he was leaving that money exclusively to me."

"And assured me that what's at Guadeluz was all mine."

"Poor Papa," murmured the touched officer. "How strange! Well, if you agree, what we should do is go to Guadeluz first and afterwards to Corchada. That way we'll dispel all doubts. What an irony it would be if there were only one."

"You're right," concurred María Josefa triumphantly. "First where I say, because you'll see that the treasure is there."

"And also because you had the good sense to speak up first, right, sister? I want you to know that I didn't say anything because I feared distressing you. You could have believed that Papa was excluding you, that I was the favorite . . . I don't know! I intended to go for the money and give you half without telling you the source. I see now that I was a fool."

"No, no, you were right," María replied, confused and embarrassed. "I'm a chatterbox, and indiscreet. That very thing should have occurred to me. I should have looked for the treasure and done what you had planned, given it to you without saying where it came from. What a lack of forethought!"

"Well, I regret that you made the first move," José responded sincerely, clasping his sister's slender fingers.

A few days later the twins made their excursion to Guadeluz and found everything exactly as María Josefa had described it. The treasure was stowed in a small, locked chest made of iron; the key didn't turn up. They loaded the chest and, giving no thought to opening it, continued their journey to Corchada, where at the foot of the demolished trunk they found another chest, also made of iron, and of the same weight and size as the first one. They took the two of them home in a single case, shut themselves up at night, and José María, armed with locksmith's tools, opened them, or rather, forced the clasps, destroying them. When the lids sprang up the amassed coins glittered, beautiful onzas and doblillas which brother and sister spilled without counting, joining the two steams of gold on the table where they mixed together like two Pactolus Rivers* that merge their wondrous waters. All of a sudden María shuddered.

"At the bottom of my chest there's a piece of paper."

"And another one in mine," her brother observed.

"It's Papa's handwriting."

"It's his writing all right."

"What does yours say?"

"Wait . . . bring the light closer . . . it says: 'My dear son, if you're reading this alone, I feel sorry for you and I forgive you, but if you're reading it in your sister's presence, I'll come out of my grave to give you my blessing."

"Mine says the very same thing," María Josefa exclaimed a moment later, sobbing and laughing at the same time.

The twins tossed the notes aside and, on top of the pile of gold, stepping on coins scattered over the carpet, extended their arms to each other and stood in an embrace for a long while.

Consolation

Teodoro was going to get married passionately in love. His fiancée and he took advantage of every possible moment to dote on one another and exhaust the sweet conversation that love intensifies through a hope soon to become a reality. The wedding would be in May if no obstacles arose on the road to the couple's happiness. But as the set date drew near, a terrible one did arise: Teodoro figured in the draw for officers and his luck was bad—his country was calling him.

Everybody knows what happens in such situations. The fiancée suffered fainting fits and attacks of hysterics, shedding tears that ran down her fresh, snow-white cheeks or that soaked her dainty lace handkerchief; and during the last few days that Teodoro was able to spend at his loved one's side, they exchanged solemn pledges of fidelity and postponed the happy event until his return. Such was his fiancée's effusive behavior that Teodoro went off with a less heavy heart, buoyed up almost continually, because he was courageous and not even mentally did he shun acceptance of duty.

Teodoro wrote whenever he could and received loving, fervent letters in response to his somewhat laconic ones which he dashed off after debilitating marches, stealing time from rest and avoiding accounts of the hardships and privations of the brutal campaign in order not to distress his loved one. A close friend, enlisted to spy on her—there isn't a man who doesn't resort to this childishness if he's very far away and truly in love—sent news that she was living in seclusion, like a widow. When he learned this, Teodoro felt a joy that made him forget about the burning thirst, the scorching sun, the airborne fever, and the thorns that tear a man's skin off.

One day, shots from a dense thicket waylaid the column that Teodoro was leading. Teodoro closed his eyes and rocked on his horse; his men came to his aid and tried to treat his wound while the invisible enemy fled in cowardly fashion. After they moved him to the hospital, it was seen that his leg bone had been smashed—a very serious compound fracture. The doctor made his decision: to save the wounded man's life it was urgent that he perform an amputation above the kneecap, and he warned that he considered it dangerous to administer chloroform to the patient. Teodoro endured the operation fully conscious, and saw how the scalpel incised his flesh and resected his muscles, how the saw bit into the bone, until reaching the marrow, and how his right leg, bloodied and lifeless now, was taken away to be buried. He neither screamed nor moaned; only in the paroxysm of pain did his teeth slice clear through the cigar in his mouth.

According to the surgeon, the operation had been an unqualified success. There was no suppuration and no fever; the stump healed well and quickly, and it didn't take Teodoro long to try out his wooden leg, a crude peg, until he could order another one from Germany that incorporated the latest advances.

Upon writing to his fiancée from the hospital he had only spoken of a wound, a minor wound. He didn't wish to afflict her or frighten her. Even so, mention of the wound alarmed the girl so much that her letters were shouts of terror and outpourings of love. Why wasn't she there to care for him and accompany him and alleviate his tortures? How was she going to bear up until his next letter in which he would inform her of his improvement?

Those tender, candid lines, which should have consoled Teodoro, caused him, on the contrary, a profound disquiet. He thought all the time that he was going to return, to see his beloved, and that she would see him too . . . But in what a state! What a difference! He was no longer the dashing officer with the trim figure and resolute, spirited bearing. He was an invalid, a pitiful invalid, a useless wretch. Good-bye marches, good-bye frisky horses, good-bye rapturous waltz, good-bye invigorating swordsmanship; he would have to live sitting down, to languish in inactivity, and receive a dole of love or of pity, given out of sympathy for his misfortune. And Teodoro, upon taking his first steps with the aid of the crutch, had a premonition of his fiancée's impression when he arrived in that condition, crippled and disabled—he, the good-looking groom-to-be whom her girl friends once coveted. To see the flicker of compassion in those cherished eyes . . . how sad it would be, how sad! He contemplated himself in the mirror and confirmed the signs of suffering on his face, and he thought about the dull noise of his peg leg on the stairs of his fiancée's home. With the back of his hand he wiped away a tear that was forming in the corner of his eye; he asked for pen and paper and wrote a short letter breaking their engagement and saying good-bye forever.

Two years went by. Teodoro had returned to the Peninsula, although not to the city where he had loved and hoped. Out of necessity he had to go there for a few days, and even though he avoided being in the streets, one afternoon he unexpectedly ran into his former fiancée, and, disconcerted and trembling, stopped and let her pass. She was walking arm in arm with a man: her husband. The amputee, recovered and steady now on his wooden leg, an orthopedic marvel expertly manufactured in Berlin that disguised his limp and ended in a splendid boot, noticed that her spouse had a ridiculous figure, bowlegged in the extreme, with bony knees and deformed feet . . . and a smile of melancholy mockery played on his serious, virile face.

The White Horse*

In a delightful garden at the entrance to heaven, St. James the Apostle was deep in meditation, his right hand supporting his leonine head of curly, parted hair the steely color of a suit of armor. He appeared to be almost as preoccupied and absorbed in thought as when, after toiling all day long in his occupation as a fisherman in the Sea of Galilee, he saw that not a single fish had fallen in his nets, but on that occasion consolation appeared to him with the arrival of the Messiah and the miracle of the fishes. Now, even though it was the fishing season, Zebedee's son, looking everywhere, was unable to divine from which direction would come the salvation, albeit a miraculous one, of those whom he loved very much.

Opposite the patron saint, in the middle of the countryside, rose a gigantic tree with an aged, wrinkled trunk and intricate foliage, but it was almost stripped of leaves, and the ones that remained were yellowish and withered. Notwithstanding the decay, it was a sylvan colossus that instilled respect, and in spite of the fact that not a few of its robust boughs were broken and torn off, the tree preserved a majestic bearing; its longevity made it venerable while its decline invited reflection on the transitory nature of grandeur. An endless number of martial arts trophies hung from the branches. There were breastplates, gorgets, helmets, greaves, and gauntlets with huge dents and cleavages made by downward blows or slashes; flamboyant swords with their points rent, and lances splintered and broken into smithereens; bucklers with arrogant mottos; snow-white cloaks emblazoned with vermilion crosses drawn, in all likelihood, with the warm blood of wounds; yataghans seized from the Moors; turbans that had been wrested along with heads; graceful banners with holes shot through them by musketry; and Boabdil's* cloak and Montezuma's picturesquely feathered diadem. Tethered to the foot of the tree by a strong iron chain was a magnificent animal, a charger bred for jousts who was luminous by dint of whiteness: the Christian Pegasus, the ideal steed that galloped across clouds and descended to earth to bring us victory.

The Apostle's eyes were glued to the horse as if he had never seen him before. He took notice of the radiant whiteness of the coat, the fluid nimbleness and exquisite undulation of the mane, the blazing pupils, the fiery breath exhaled through the nostrils, the slenderness of the legs as delicate as a woman's ankles, and the appearance of electricity given off by the brave, celestial animal's body. Simply by reason of seeing that his rider of yore was looking at him, the horse shuddered and raised his ears; he breathed deeply and pawed at the earth with his shining hoof and seemed to say in sign language: 'When will the time come? Are we always going to be like this? Why don't you untie me? Why don't we, between flashes of light and sparks, once more cross the red firmament, the air inflamed with pitched battles?'

The warrior Apostle stood and went to caress his mount's back. He wanted to console him, moderate his impatience, but did not know how, because he, a glorious veteran, also dreamed incessantly of renewing the feats of other times. No doubt to increase his anxiety and revive his memory, there appeared nearby a soul who had evidently just entered Paradise, for he gave clear signs of not knowing his way around and of being disoriented and uncertain of himself. The newcomer was a dark-complexioned, shriveled up, and gaunt man of medium height; wrapped around his body were remnants of a yellow and red* cloth, all of which was quickly equalized in hue by the blood that was flowing from several mortal wounds. St. James ran towards the brave man with open arms, and the Spaniard, on seeing before him the patron saint of his homeland, fell to his knees and kissed the Apostle's feet with infinite tenderness.

"Boanerges,* son of thunder," he murmured devoutly, "why have you abandoned us? In our misfortune we relied on you. We were hoping that you would order lightning to strike our enemies or rain heavenly fire on them, like the fire that you wished to hurl against those Samaritans who closed the gates of their city to Jesus. Look, St. James, what has happened to us. I'll say it to you in the words of the Gospel that is read on your feast day: we have become a spectacle for nations, angels, and mankind. We have hit bottom. And all because of your absence, Apostle of combat. Untie your charger, guide him through the air, put yourself at our head. The white horse smells battle. Don't you hear how he neighs, desirous of breaking into a run at the shout of 'Close in on them, Spain?' Go down: they're waiting for you 'there.' The land that believed itself invincible because of you awaits your coming. The steed wants to break his chain. St. James! Good St. James! My lord St. James!"

On hearing such urgent entreaties, the Apostle was even more moved. To let loose his white charger, go off at a gallop, wield again his flaming sword! He had been yearning to do just that for so long! Not by choice was he mired in inaction with his mount chained to the tree and his battlefield arms hanging from the branches. Raising and consoling the Spaniard, and embracing him, St. James began to bandage his bloody wounds; after he had finished, he went to the tree and untied his white steed. Wild with joy on seeing himself free and assuming that the adventures of other times would return, the animal shook his head, tossed his mane, curveted gracefully, and beating the dust with his burnished hooves, stirred up a little golden cloud. For his part, the patron saint was taking down his coat of mail and putting it on; he was adjusting the large, wide hat trimmed with fluted shells; he was securing his cloak around his shoulders; and he was fastening his shield to his left arm and girding his baldric and the dreadful sword. In the meantime, the Spaniard was placing on the horse the saddle embroidered in gold relief, the bridle, and the breast collar that was incrusted with polished, uncut precious stones. And just when the Apostle was in the act of steadying his foot in the silver stirrup to mount up, from the neighboring forest there appeared another Spaniard, dressed in plain, brown cloth and wearing coarse, leather sandals, motioning to the Apostle to stop. St. James waited; in the peasant with the sunburned complexion and the rustic dress, he had just recognized St. Isidore,* an unpretentious, hardworking day laborer who in his life had never ridden anything other than donkeys laden with wheat because he led them to the mill.

"Order of the Lord!" he cried out in exaggerated fashion. "Order of the Lord! We need that horse to harness him to the plow and help us till farmland. And that Spaniard over there, let him come to carry the yoke. You know very well, Boanerges, what the Lord said on a memorable occasion when your mother petitioned Him for you and your brother the highest place in heaven: 'Those who wish to be above all others, let them first drink from my cup.' My fellow countryman, let's plow patiently and without wasting a moment."

Scissors

"Marriage," Fr. Baltar was saying as he took part without a hint of intransigence in a rather secular discussion, "marriage . . . is like a pair of scissors."

"Like scissors, Father?" exclaimed one of those present, showing his surprise. "Are you aware that it's a novel comparison?"

"More than novel, fitting," declared the priest, refusing with a gesture a second glass of Riga kümmel. "Scissors, as you all know, are an instrument made up of two equal parts, or very similar parts, joined by a pin and rivet of the same metal. Even though each blade of the scissors is sharp and well-tempered, if the pin is missing . . . the scissors are useless. But joined by that rivet, they can create marvels and cut divinely the cloth of life."

"Understood," said another man in the group listening to the priest (a man who was knowledgeable, somewhat glib and distrustful). "You have only to tell us if you believe that superior scissors abound."

"Usually, items of superior quality never abound, or at least we're so hard to please that they always seem to be in short supply," responded with a smile that evangelical and at the same time (lovely combination!) cultured man. "Although the mystery of marriage consists of the pin, the quality of the two halves is also very important. Go into a shop and ask for scissors. They'll bring out two dozen for you, all seemingly equal, all the same price. Only by taking the two dozen pairs to your home and using them would you be able to make the right choice—that is, through use you discover the nature of the scissors. Seamstresses are so convinced of this that any pair of scissors that 'works' for them they wouldn't trade for an ounce of gold. I've found scissors made of gold! And why is this so remarkable? An example of natural love, purified by divine law! I'm going to relate to you an instance that I observed with my own eyes, one that moved me

115

deeply, even though it's no more than an ordinary drama, and its players, plain, common people.

"While at the monastery of S*** recovering from a fever that I picked up in Tangiers, a fever that I couldn't shake, I had the opportunity of meeting, amongst many other families, a married couple, shopkeepers who dealt in assorted cloths, flannels and cottons. Their place of business was in the arcade of the old square, not far from the cathedral. I wasn't their confessor—their parish priest was—but they liked to consult me as a friend. The woman's name was Doña Consuelo and the husband's was Don Andrés. Well-off and well-suited to each other, they would have been happy if they hadn't had a troublemaker of a son who married and embarrassed them night and day. Quarrelsome, depraved, and spendthrift, neither his mother's tears, nor his father's reprimands, nor the exhortations which, at their request, I made to him several times, moved him to give up a single one of his vices. And so, in view of the fact that the young fellow seemed incorrigible, my advice was to send him to a faraway land where necessity and lack of support would force him to mend his ways.

"The idea suited the father fine, and even the mother realized that it was the only recourse. And as the outcast chose Manila, off to Manila he was sent, with very urgent letters of recommendation for the rector of one of our order's monasteries.

"Six months later I began to receive welcome news concerning the conduct of my protégé, who was being praised for his industriousness and his cleverness. He was turning over a new leaf. The old people, when they heard about it, were beside themselves with joy. The rector was the one who sent me such glad tidings since the young fellow wasn't in the habit of writing.

"Some time went by in this way until one day the rector's letter brought not good news but terrible news: Don Andrés's son had been stabbed to death in a fight while coming out of a cockpit. I was charged with informing the parents.

"The mission was a sad one, but our lives are surrounded by sadness, and judging that the father would bear up better at first than the mother, I summoned Don Andrés to my cell. Preparing him as best I could for the bitter pill, I gave him the news. He wasn't slow in understanding. On the contrary, he seemed to have an inkling of what was coming. He construed 'death' from *wounds* as soon as I alluded to them. He didn't cry, but the expression on his face was like that of the criminal who finds himself at the stairs of the scaffold when the prison gates are opened (and I use this analogy because I've attended to a number of unfortunate offenders in their last moments).

"When Don Andrés was able to breathe freely, he crossed his hands and said: 'Father, I have to ask you a big favor. Between the two of us, let's keep Consuelo from learning what has happened. Just a few years ago my wife was robust, in good health, but this grief over our son has broken her. She'll be sixty soon and she's suffering from a serious illness, a type of consumption. If she learns of this misfortune, she'll go right away. If we prevent her from knowing that the boy has been killed, maybe she'll last a little longer (they called him the 'boy' even though he was past twenty-seven). I'll foot the bill of all the expenses run up over there—funeral, legal costs. And I forgive the murderers from the bottom of my heart, but I don't want Consuelo to find out.'

"Was I right or wrong in agreeing? I don't know. From the depths of my soul I wanted to indulge that miserable man. Every two or three weeks I went to the shop with fabricated letters, supposedly received from Manila, that spoke of their absent son and praised his progress at work, his reliability, and his integrity.

"Doña Consuelo, whose health was deteriorating visibly, coughed incessantly and suffered from constant fatigue, but she revived on hearing those favorable reports, praised them with puerile extremes, and demanded that Don Andrés share her joy.

"'Do you see, Andrés, how much we have to be grateful for to San Antonio?' she would exclaim with eyes glazed from weeping that I attributed to an excess of happiness. 'Do you see what good fortune? Our boy has changed. He's behaving honorably. After he spends a few years there he'll return and we'll put him in charge of our business. Fr. Baltar, I'm going to give you some money to be delivered to him over there. We know what it's like to be young, and I don't want my son to be in need of anything.'

"And her husband, drowning his sorrows, his face turning blue, would reply: 'All right, woman. Bring Father those thirty *duros* . . . but for that you don't have to get so emotional. How silly!'

"You had to feel sorry for them. The mother was giving me *duros* for her son to enjoy, and the father was secretly requesting of me that they be invested in the salvation of his soul.

"I didn't deviate from my role in the slightest because I saw Doña Consuelo getting worse. With each passing day the blow of her son's death would have been more dangerous. Don Andrés, either fearful of an indiscretion on my part or not wanting to leave his sick wife's side, was always present when I went to spend time with them. I would find them together like birds perched on the same branch, huddled side by side to ward off the cold: she, coughing and insisting that 'it was nothing' and he, purplish, half-asphyxiated, asthmatic, but exerting himself to joke with his wife and even flirt with her, which in other circumstances might have struck me as comical and laughable, but which in those touched me deeply.

"And on we went with the farce of the letters, which produced such an effect on the poor mother that I even thought I noticed her motioning to me when her husband wasn't looking at us— motioning out of approval, supplication, gratitude. I interpreted her gestures like this: 'Even if the boy does something foolish, keep telling Andrés that he's behaving like an angel.' All this was supposition on my part, because I repeat—I never spent time alone with Doña Consuelo.

"One evening I was summoned at a very late hour. Don Andrés came to tell me that his wife was dying or was close to dying, that she had the whim of making her confession to me, and that it was essential to invent a letter announcing the 'boy's' imminent arrival. 'Let's see if this way we can keep her going for a few days,' he added, trembling so much that I couldn't refuse him this last favor.

"I had barely entered Doña Consuelo's room when she glanced at her husband and Don Andrés left, but not without making an expressive gesture by way of cautioning and imploring me. I approached the sick woman's bed—she was moving her lips rapidly, as if she were praying. I sat down at the head of it and spoke those affectionate phrases that are like ladlefuls of balm and which we say as a matter of course to the dying, but I was very taken aback when she turned her face to me—a face that shone with gratitude—while taking my hand to kiss it.

"'Fr. Baltar,' she said, 'may God repay you for all the time that you've been deceiving my husband. Promise me that you won't disabuse him after I die!'"

"'What are you saying? Deceiving him?' I asked, thinking that she was raving from weakness and fever."

"'If it weren't for you,' she went on, ignoring my questions, 'Andrés would be dying too because he would know about our boy . . . I hope he never finds out!'"

"'About the boy?' I exclaimed, remembering my pledge to Don Andrés. 'The boy's perfectly all right, he's on his way, and will be here soon to embrace you.'"

"'Sure I'll embrace him . . . in the next life. Don't trouble yourself on my account. I knew about it right away, I even felt it in my bones. Do you think I didn't have somebody over there entrusted with writing to me everything that happened to my son? The letters were addressed to one of my women friends; that way Andrés couldn't discover if anything bad came his way. And since I had written to Fr. Rector asking him that my husband be told only the good and happy things, when you came with those made-up letters saying that the boy was still alive and working, I helped you deceive my poor Andrés, who's not at all well, and who shouldn't be distressed . . . It's been hard for me to pretend, Father, because in all these years of marriage I've never kept anything else from him . . .'"

The priest ended his story at this point and, looking around, saw our faces lit up with a deeply felt empathy.

"So both of them knew and each concealed it from the other! What inner drama!" exclaimed the man who had spoken first.

"About those scissors, Father," said the skeptic, "you can certainly affirm that they were made of pure gold, with diamond inlay."

"I can affirm that I've seen them open in the shape of a cross," the priest responded pointedly.

The Lady Bandit*

Those who consider women frail creatures and equate bravery and leadership with the masculine sex should have become acquainted with the renowned Pepona, and learned about her, not what is recorded in the dusty files of the court clerk's legal proceedings, but the vivid, vibrant reality.

Women have been concubines, harborers of fugitives, and thieves' spies; they've been on the lookout to warn men and at home to hide them; and they've even aided and consorted with them; but Pepona performed none of these subordinate roles, for she was, indisputably, captain of a numerous and well-organized band of robbers.

I never did manage to find out what Pepona's first moves were —how she *debuted* in the profession for which she felt an inspired calling. When I met her, the fairs and roads of two provinces were already the arena of her feats. I wouldn't want you to picture Pepona in a false, romantic way, wearing an Andalusian hat with upturned brim set at a rakish angle and carrying a blunderbuss after Carmen, not even with a knife concealed between her blouse and the reed bodice worn at that time by the village women in my native region. It is known, on the contrary, that the lady bandit never in her life wielded a weapon other than a goad, which she used to prod oxen and the shaggy hack that she rode. What was her and the band's business? Robbing? Then do it in a big way, but without creating a scandal, or causing harm. This approach did not stem from soft-heartedness on her part, but from very astute reasoning to avoid a dangerous course that could lead to the gallows.

Pepona's tactic was as follows: like an honest housekeeper of the Count of Borrajeiros or the Marquis of Ulloa, she would go to the fair on her pony, carrying a large basket for purchases. At the fair, members of her band were already awaiting her, similarly disguised as peaceful peasants. While buying a distaff, an oil-lamp or a pound of flax, Pepona would observe the traders attentively, and her spies, in taverns, kept watch on deals that were closed with a glass of old wine. Informed of where the man who had just sold the pair of oxen was heading and that he was going home with gold stashed inside his belt, the band of robbers would go on ahead to await him at a lonely, suitable spot. They usually blackened their faces or put on black cloth masks. Pepona didn't take part; she would look on, hiding behind a clump of trees. If she intervened it was to prevent the band from mistreating or killing someone and to leave the *consolation*, a small sum that a few highwaymen grant their victims so they can buy drink en route.

The authorities were lenient toward Pepona, who enjoyed cordial relations with judges, prosecutors, and attorneys, as well as with the rural aristocracy. She was a shrewd diplomat who never once attempted a holdup of castles or manor houses—just the reverse of Andalusian bandits. A profound difference in types! Pepona only robbed unfortunate carriers, muleteers or peasants who were taking payments in kind to their masters.

Oh! It was better to have Pepona as a friend than an enemy, a fact well appreciated by the only somewhat upper social class for whom the captain professed sworn hatred. The truth of the matter is that this class has always suffered persecution at the hands of thieves, at least in Galicia. I'm referring to the clergy. Priests were believed, and are still believed, to be given to hiding savings in their straw mattresses, and all count has been lost of how many times bandits have roasted their feet and spattered them with boiling oil. Nevertheless, something particular was noticed in Pepona—a fury difficult to explain, the source of which gave rise to endless conjecture. The fact is that Pepona, normally so merciful, was fiercely cruel to priests, and perhaps they were the ones who tacked onto her name the epithet "Wolf Lady."

Terror, therefore, was rife among the clergy, who would venture to appear at pilgrimages and fairs only if well-armed and with an escort, when a young, inexperienced priest happened to take over the parish at Treselle—a pleasant, friendly priest whom the archbishop recommended highly to all the prominent citizens within a radius of ten leagues. On learning, from conversations in the sacristy, of the danger that those of his calling faced in Pepona, the new priest smiled and said softly, with a certain subtle irony:

"Why do you make so much of her? Why are you afraid of a woman? Men afraid of a woman!"

His companions could scarcely believe their ears. They pounced on him like a pack of rabid hounds. What if he took on the Wolf Lady since he was so brave and unconcerned? What if they told him to go parade his bravado somewhere else? Let him tangle with the band of robbers and their captain and they'd fry him in oil! Did he think the rest of them were a bunch of little sissies or what?

"I won't take on the entire band," the youth said when the uproar died down, "because of the saying that two Moors can best one Christian, but as far as the Wolf Lady herself is concerned . . . what the heck, man-to-man. . ."

From that day on Treselle's cleric was considered boastful and foolish, and he became the butt of practical jokes which took on an aggressive character at the August 15th fair. The argument occurred during dessert, after a meal at Micaela's inn in Cebre where they serve an outstanding old wine and a monumental stew of pork sausage, ham, and ear. The priests had decided to sleep there and not return to their homes until the following day, with an escort, because Pepona was seen hanging around the fair. Their upset young colleague from Treselle then exclaimed on dipping his last biscuit in his glass of sweet wine:

"Well, just to show you . . . I'm no braggart, but I'm capable right now of taking off all alone for my rectory. Hey, Micaela! Have them saddle my mount!"

A few minutes afterwards, his spirited little chestnut mare with plump hindquarters was waiting at the inn's door. Saying goodbye to his startled fellow diners, the priest mounted and disappeared at a trot. Mother of Mercy! What he was getting himself into! The impetuosity of youth! He'd learn, he'd learn.

Ashamed, several fellow clergymen repeated:

"Somebody should have accompanied him."

But nobody did. It was his funeral—for bragging about being so brave!

The sun was going down, and the young priest felt a tightness in his chest while passing by the last houses in Cebre; looking around suspiciously, he reined in his mare. His cheeks, red from arguing earlier, were now pale. He was becoming unnerved. 'I acted unwisely, but I can't back down. I'm afraid,' he mused, 'and I need to compose myself.' He touched the holsters on his saddletree; he carried two magnificent English pistols, a gift from the Marquis of Ulloa. Inside his shirt he felt the shape of a knife used for cutting tobacco. He recovered his calm then and studied the lay of the land. The road was deserted and the wind howled mournful refrains in the tall pines.

The cleric spurred his mount. At the bend where the road turns and barren crags tower above it, a tall, burly figure suddenly appeared. The mare stopped, pricking her ears. It was a brawny woman, leaning on a goad. She seemed to be begging because her left hand was outstretched, but the priest, who had been a student, saw that what the supposed beggar woman was doing was making an indecent gesture. He reacted energetically, stirred by indignation.

He swiftly drew a pistol from the saddletree and cocked it. The woman jumped, and on her tanned face, illuminated by the last rays of the western sun, a kind of animal terror was depicted —the fright of the wolf caught in the trap. The cleric couldn't figure out the cause of this phenomenon, a strange one in the captain. Convinced that there were no priests or carriers who would dare leave Cebre alone at that hour, the lady bandit had given her band of robbers leave until the following morning, and was heading home. On seeing a dandy of a young priest who risked being on the road, she had decided to play a dirty trick on him, but the noise of the trigger caused her to tremble and persuaded her that flight was her only recourse. She leaped sideways toward the pine grove, and the cleric, spurring his spirited mare, went after her, caught up with her, and sent her sprawling. He sprang from his mount, clutching the pistol, but the Wolf Lady, without giving him time to do a thing, wrapped her arms around his legs from the very ground on which she lay and managed to knock him over. She wrested the pistol from him and threw it at the hedgerow; then she grabbed his neck with her strong, rough hands and squeezed and squeezed.

Pine grove, sky, and air all changed color for the hapless cleric.

First he saw everything red, then big purple and violet rings danced in front of his eyes, which were popping out of their sockets. It wasn't him, it wasn't his reasoning; it was pure instinct that guided his right hand in search of the knife concealed inside his shirt. And while the Wolf Lady split her sides laughing obscenely at the spectacle of the priest sticking his tongue out, his hand plunged the blade blindly. The captain's terrible iron grip loosened and she fell backwards, stabbed in the chest.

Bandits have a strong constitution. The Wolf Lady recovered, but her spirit was broken, her prestige undermined, and her legend destroyed. Pepona overcome by a sissy of a young priest! And the new captain general who came to Montañosa—a bad-tempered veteran—pursued the band so relentlessly that the priests were able to return in peace, even at nightfall, to their rectories.

The Nurse

The patient uttered a pitiful moan, turning over painfully in his bed, and his wife, who was resting on a sofa in the adjoining sitting room, sat up with a start and hurried solicitously to where her duty called her.

It was an arresting sight: a woman whose beauty showed signs of fading from the sleepless nights of the long vigil; a woman with chestnut hair and dark rings around black eyes that gleamed from the feverish excitement that consumed her; a woman holding up her husband's body, offering him a spoonful of the potion that relieved his acute pains. It was a family scene, a glimpse into sacrosanct feelings, of the kind that persist long after the disappearance of physical attraction and dreams, nature's eternal lure for mortals. Undoubtedly the patient thought of something similar, which was what would occur to a spectator watching the two of them, and when he had swallowed the dosage, he sought her thin, shaky hand, and on feeling it, brought it to his lips in a gesture of touching gratitude.

"How do you feel now?" she asked, gently plumping his pillows.

"Better . . . A moment ago I couldn't stand it any longer. When do you suppose God will take pity on me?"

"Don't say that, Federico," the nurse murmured earnestly.

"Bah!" he insisted. "Don't worry. I heard it with my own ears. The doctor told you yesterday at the door, when both of you thought me drowsy, which doesn't prevent hearing. I'm glad, dear Juana. Don't take away my only hope. The sooner this hell comes to an end . . . No, forgive me! Juana, I forgot that an angel is at my side. Because, oh, if it weren't for you . . . !"

Juana may have been saintly, but she did not, strictly speaking, have an angelic countenance. On the contrary, her face revealed features of a certain hardness, a tenseness at the corners of the mouth, a gloomy air in the premature wrinkles on her forehead

125

and, above all, in her expression. Federico was moved thinking about the ravages wreaked on her beauty in the fight against his horrible illness.

"Juana," he faltered. "I feel a little calmer now. Undoubtedly you've increased the dosage of the sedative. Don't be startled. I'd be grateful to you! Listen . . . I'm going to take advantage of this time. I have to tell you. Promise you'll listen to me without getting upset, Juana."

"Federico, don't talk. Don't tire yourself," she responded. "Don't think about anything except your health. Save the rest for later, when you've recovered completely."

"Later!" the patient repeated pensively, and his wandering, blurred gaze settled on an imaginary point in space—far off, far off . . . in the direction of the mysterious *later* toward which his destiny inexorably dragged him. "Now," he insisted. "Now or never, Juana. It won't do me any harm, believe me. I'm certain that it will, on the contrary, do me good. If you suspected the heartache a secret causes! If you knew how oppressive it is to keep quiet all the time!"

"A secret?" Juana echoed him, turning pale.

"Please, darling. Don't be alarmed already, and don't get excited afterwards, when I confess to you . . . Promise me you'll be calm. Sit down here. Give me your hand. No? As you wish."

"Do you see? You're tiring yourself. Drop it, Federico," Juana persisted, agitated by an imperceptible tremor, as if she were struggling with herself.

"Listen, I know better than anybody what a bad light it puts me in. I'm certain that even to accept death with more resignation I need to unbosom myself, to admit to it. Juana, right now we're only a miserable patient and a saintly nurse who's caring for him. I'm asking you for the final consolation; be indulgent; tell me beforehand that you'll forgive me."

"I forgive you . . . and stop talking, Federico!" she muttered quietly, and angrily, to her regret.

Making a superhuman effort, he sat up in bed, sticking out his chest and leaning toward his wife in a loving, humble display of bliss. He was one of those patients sensitized by pain who do and say tender, heartrending things and strive to excite the feelings of those around him. Juana's profound emotion encouraged him, and crossing his hands in fervent supplication, he started speaking all at once.

"You forgive me, you forgive me ... It's because you don't understand; it's because you believe that it has to do with a minor transgression. It was serious. I'm very much at fault, and it torments me to think that I'm robbing not only the time and effort that you take in caring for me, but something else more valuable. After you know, will you still love me? You won't abandon me, leaving me to die like a dog?"

Juana bounded to her feet. The nervous tremor in her body was becoming more pronounced. Her voice was hoarse, gloomy, funereal, when she said with seeming ironic coldness:

"Save yourself the trouble of confessing. I'm almost as much in the know as you are."

Federico, taken by surprise, let himself fall back on the pillow. His eyes glazed over without becoming watery—the dry tears, so to speak, of worn out organisms.

"You knew!"

"Well, what did you think?" she replied, livid, gritting her teeth and looking daggers at him.

Federico covered his face, gripped by terror. The only thing that was sustaining him had just crumbled inside. He believed in his nurse's love; he was still recovering, thanks to this conviction, when Juana's tone of voice, expression, and attitude suddenly snatched away from him this sacred belief. Hatred had shown through so openly in them, was so impetuous in its unexpected disclosure, that the sharp sensation of danger—of latent, ill-defined, watchful danger—suppressed at that instant the notion of remorse and checked the confession on his lips.

"Juana," he sighed, "come, listen to me. Look, nothing happened. What I was going to tell you was of no great importance!"

She approached him. Her jet-black eyes were flashing; a tragic frown knitted her brow; her nostrils quivered from fury. Federico had never seen her like that, and, nonetheless, it was an expression that adapted itself well to the character of her physiognomy or, rather, revealed her real physiognomy. The patient's terror paralyzed even his tongue. On a childish impulse, he tried to duck under the covers.

"Don't hide," she articulated contemptuously, trampling him

with her tone. "Look, if I see you so afraid, I'll laugh at you. Do you understand? I'll laugh at you. And it's all I needed to make my revenge complete! To laugh! Laughter! Oh, how I detest you! I wouldn't keep quiet any longer . . ."

Federico was looking at her, bewildered and crazed. Could he be having a nightmare? Was this death already, the ugly face of death, damnation, punishment from beyond the grave? Was it the form that his sinner's conscience took to torture him?

"Juana!" he stammered. "Am I dreaming? Revenge? You detest me?"

She drew nearer, brought her face close to his, and letting her words sink in slowly, repeated:

"I detest you. You thought me a lamb. I'm a tigress, a tigress, not a lamb. You wronged me and betrayed me and offended me; you tortured my spirit, you drove me crazy, you nourished me with gall and wormwood, and you didn't even take the trouble to acknowledge that my youth was withering away, my beauty fading and that my spirit, so trusting and generous before, was becoming corrupt. And when you found yourself at death's door, death, yes, and soon—you guessed it—then you called me: 'Juana, be my nurse . . . Juana, give me the potion . . .'"

"And you did it in sublime fashion, Juana!" he sobbed. "You've been a martyr at my bedside. Don't deny it, my darling! Forgive me!"

Juana guffawed. Her laughter was a nervous fit; it resembled a convulsion that tangled her in a knot.

"Yes, I did," she repeated at last, controlling herself through sheer will power. "Yes, I did. I indeed did give the potion to you. Every day I gave it to you . . . , the one that would do you the most damage! That particular one and none other! Oh! You didn't suspect it? You're the one who's really been deceived! You! You!"

Soft knocks on the door were heard. The servant's respectful voice announced:

"The doctor."

And the affable young physician, clean shaven and wearing gloves, came in, asking from the threshold:

"How's the patient doing? And his incomparable nurse?"

The Cuff Link

The Countess of Noroña made a gesture of annoyance when she received and read the urgent note of invitation. Since her husband's death two and a half years ago, she had been in a state between mourning and relief, and had not attended any social functions. In part because of genuine sorrow, in part because of convenience, she had become accustomed to not going out evenings, to retiring early, to not dressing up, and to disregarding the world and its pomps; she devoted herself to Diego, her beloved and only son. Nevertheless, there's no rule without an exception: the invitation was to Carlota's wedding, her favorite niece, her goddaughter.

'And the worst part is that they've moved up the date,' she thought. 'They're getting married on the sixteenth . . . Today is the tenth . . . We'll see tomorrow if Pastiche can get me out of this predicament. Certainly in a week he can sew my lacework on gray or violet satin. I don't require a lot of fripperies. With my lacework and my jewelry . . .'

She rang the bell and several minutes later the maid came along.

"What were you doing?" asked the countess, impatient.

"I was helping Gregorio search for something that the young master has lost."

"And what thing is that?"

"A cuff link. One of the garnet pair that the countess gave him a month ago."

"God help me! What children! To lose already such a beautiful and original cuff link! There's none like them in Madrid. Very well! You can continue searching later. Right now bring my Chantilly lace, flounces, and bertha from the main closet. I don't know on what shelf I could've put them. Look around."

The maid obeyed, not without making for her part that involuntary face of surprise provoked in longtime domestic servants by unexpected orders that signal a variation in the routine. After the girl withdrew, the countess entered the spacious bedroom and removed from her secretaire a key ring with small keys to unlock an Empire-period escritoire-bureau, of the type that when the front is lowered it converts into a writing table and inside has a well-built set of drawers. She opened it, thinking to herself: 'Luckily I removed them from the bank this winter . . . I was afraid that something of this sort might come up.'

Upon inserting the key in one of the drawers, she noticed with surprise that it was unlocked.

"Is it possible that I left it like this?" she murmured, almost out loud.

It was the first drawer on the left. The countess thought that she had put in it her big diamond eglantine brooch shaped like a branch. But it only contained worthless trinkets, a few enamel watches, and crumpled pieces of tissue paper. Anxious and apprehensive, she went on to examine the remaining drawers. All of them were open; two were splintered and had smashed locks. The countess's hands were trembling and she broke out in a cold sweat. There could be no doubt: all the jewelry was missing from the escritoire, both family heirlooms and wedding pieces. The diamond eglantine, strings of pearls, a necklace of mounted stones, a diamond and ruby brooch . . . Stolen! Stolen!

A strange sensation, familiar to those who have found themselves in a similar situation, came over the countess. For an instant she doubted her memory, she doubted the actual existence of the objects she wasn't seeing. Then her precise, categorical recollection immediately prevailed. She even remembered that when wrapping the ruby brooch in tissue paper and raw cotton she had noticed that it looked tarnished, and that it was necessary to take it to the jeweler to have it cleaned. 'Well, the escritoire-bureau was securely locked on the outside,' reasoned the countess, in whose spirit, faced with the crime committed against it, there was being set in motion the process of inquiry that even without wanting to we carry out. 'A house thief. Someone who comes and goes freely at any hour; who takes advantage of carelessness on my part to lay hands on my keys; who can spend time here trying them . . . Someone who knows as well as

I do where I keep my jewelry, and knows its value and my habit of not wearing it these last few years.'

Like dispersed rays of light that join together and form a powerful beam, these observations converged on one name:

"Lucía!"

It was she. It couldn't be anyone else. The promptings of doubt and the high regard in which she held her didn't offset the overwhelming evidence. True, Lucía had been serving very faithfully in her home for eight years. The daughter of honest tenants of the countess and raised under the protection of the Noroña family, her loyalty was proved by nursing the master and mistress through serious illnesses, when she had spent entire weeks without going to bed, keeping watch at night, and sacrificing her youth and her health with the easy generosity of humble people. 'But,' the countess mused, 'it's possible to be very loyal, very docile, even unselfish . . . and one day yield to the temptation of greed, the ruler over all other instincts. There's a reason for keys, bolts, and strongboxes in this world; there's a reason why we always keep an eye on the poor man when chance or circumstances put him in contact with the treasures of the rich man . . .' In the countess's mind, influenced by the powerful impression of the discovery, her image of Lucía was changing—a psychic phenomenon of the most curious sort. The traits of the kind, innocent maid, a model of self-denial, were being erased, and there appeared a cunning, astute, greedy woman who awaited, hardened by hypocrisy, the moment to stretch out her thieving hands and make off with the contents of her mistress's jewel case.

'That's why the rascal was startled when I instructed her to bring the lacework,' thought the countess, yielding to the human instinct of explaining any act in the light of the dominant concern. 'She feared that when I needed the lacework I would need the jewelry too. That has to be it! Just you wait, you'll get what's coming to you. I don't want to start bickering with her. If I see her crying, I'll probably take pity on her, and if I give her time to ask my forgiveness, I may be foolish enough to grant it to her. Before I get over my anger, the message.'

The countess, tremulous and furious, scribbled in pencil—on the very writing board of the bureau-escritoire—a few words on a card, put it inside an envelope which she addressed, and hit the bell twice; when Gregorio, the valet, appeared at the door, she handed him the message.

"This goes to the police station, right now."

Alone once more, the countess contemplated the drawers again.

'The girl's a strong thief,' she thought, looking at the two drawers that had been opened forcibly. 'Undoubtedly in her haste she didn't find the right key for each one and forced them. Since I leave the house so infrequently and spend all my time in that sitting room . . .'

Upon hearing Lucía's approaching footsteps, the countess's anger speeded up the flow of her blood which, as the saying goes, boiled. The girl entered carrying a flat cardboard box.

"I had a lot of trouble finding them, my lady. They were on the highest shelf between the satin bedspreads and the mantillas."

At first the countess didn't respond. She was breathing deeply so her voice wouldn't sound agitated and hoarse. She had a bitter taste in her mouth, a swarm of insults was on the tip of her tongue, and she experienced an urge to grab the servant girl by the arm and throw her against the wall. If a sum of money equivalent in value to the jewelry had been stolen from her, she wouldn't be seething with so much wrath; but this was family jewelry, the splendor and respectability of their ancestry . . . and touching those pieces was a transgression, an outrage.

The voice can be controlled, the tongue held, the hands immobilized . . . but not the eyes. The countess's stare, terrible and accusatory, sought Lucía's eyes and found them fixed, as if she were hypnotized, on the bureau-escritoire, still open with the drawers pulled out. In a tone of surprise, of happy, spontaneous surprise, the maid exclaimed, while taking a closer look:

"My lady! My lady! There . . . in that small drawer of the escritoire . . . The missing cuff link! Master Diego's cuff link!"

The countess opened her mouth, spread her arms, and understood . . . without understanding. Then all of a sudden she stiffened and fell backwards, unconscious, her heart almost broken.

Rescue

On his way to the pit, as dawn was just beginning to break, Ramón Luis gave rein to his bitterness. His wife, his Rosario, to be unfaithful to him, to dishonor him like that! And he didn't even have the consolation of uncertainty. He had clearly seen that damned Camilo Solines leave by the poultry yard gate, hiding as he went. Surprise had frozen him, and he didn't grab the bastard by the scruff of the neck to choke him, as he should have. It was true; Ramón believed, as if it were a law that urgently compelled him, that he had to kill Rosario's lover. Because she . . . she already bore, as a lesson, some good marks on her body. But what more can be done by the man who has four children, all of them small enough to fit underneath one large basket? No, no; he had to pay, the thief had to pay. He'd catch him at the bottom of the mine, by some dark turns, and there, with no other weapon, without even picking up a piece of slate, just with his bare fists . . . At the first faint light of dawn, Ramón looked at his black, hardened hands that coal dust had scraped smooth of hair, and his fingers twitched thinking about his enemy's slender throat. A punk like him, a son of a bitch like him! And for him a woman loses all sense of shame, forgets about her children! What if his fellow workers knew about it? So much the better, let them know; then they'd find out that nobody messes with Ramón Luis.

The miner arrived late. When he entered the huge shed to pick up his lamp, a cluster of men blocked the way. Confused exclamations came from the group, the anguish of a catastrophe. He made inquiries.

"A cave-in. No one knows how many are trapped. We're waiting for the engineer."

In their ascent from tunnels and pits miners came on the run, knocking each other down in a rush of terror, anxious to convince themselves that they weren't the ones who had been trapped down below. The collapse was tremendous. Undoubt-edly every tunnel of the southern side of the mine, or at least the greater part of them, was blocked up. The engineer had now arrived, the collar of his sleeveless smock frock turned up over his cheeks, which were pale from sleep and cold. He was young, energetic, and high-strung, and gave decisive orders.

"Don't waste a minute. Begin at the tunnel on the left."

"There's a chance that they've taken refuge there," an old fore-man murmured. "But they're probably ground to pulp ... squashed by the equipment."

The rescue work commenced, somewhat disorderly at first, but in time becoming quiet, well-organized, and methodical. The res-cuers held out no hope; the fatality of the event crushed them too. A distracted Ramón Luis was doing very little. The foreman got the attention of the work gang.

"Hey! Come on, come on! Remember there are men trapped in there!"

At noon women and dirty children in ragged clothing—the rabble who live off coal—began to turn up. Before ascertaining if their loved ones were buried in the depths of the earth, the former were already weeping and wailing.

"Let's call the roll," the engineer ordered. "Let's find out once and for all how many are missing!"

On hearing the order, Ramón Luis's heart gave a sudden start. Shall we lay odds that the bastard, the one who had branded him with dishonor, was one of the men buried alive? Because look who was coming, shuffling and sobbing—his bitch of a mother, Juaneca, who as a girl had taken a turn with all the boys. In distress she kept repeating:

"My son! My son! My precious son!"

Oh! Surely, surely the troublemaker was at the bottom of the caved-in tunnel, his head mashed, his legs broken, his ribs cracked ...

The hand of God strikes in untold ways! And a frenzied joy shook the wronged husband, who laughed alone, as if in spite of himself. The recount confirmed his wish: seventeen were miss-ing, and among them Camilo Solines, the little miner, which was what the girls called him.

His mother, throwing herself to the ground, clawed at it, as if she wished to break it apart and free her son. Standing up, she then confronted the workers:

"Get him out of there! Lazy good-for-nothings, what are you doing that you're not digging faster? Don't you see that he's trapped with nothing to eat? Not a drop of water to drink? My son? Get him out, you rotten Christians, you!"

Ramón Luis, as if the invective were directed solely at him, involuntarily grasped his shovel and began to work quickly. From time to time he thought: 'He's rotting in there; good, let him rot . . . He's probably in hell already.' Behind the miner rose the voice of the mother, passionate and irate:

"Get him out of there!"

An impulse made Ramon Luis turn around—he wanted to shout too: 'He's not alive, he'll turn up mashed to a pulp; and if by chance he is alive, I'll kill him, do you understand?' But on seeing the mother's face, sublime with rage and love, the aggrieved husband lowered his eyes. His shovel resounded again, striking the earth, asking: "Where are they?"

Hours went by, then days. The feverish excitement of the mother, that she-wolf defender of her cub who neither ate nor slept and was kept on her feet by slugs of brandy, infected the rescuers. Ramón Luis was the only discouraged one.

"They're dead," he would say in an undertone. "There's no point in breaking our backs. They're dead as a doornail."

A buzz greeted his words, and an unconscious fatigue gripped the miners.

On the fifth day, at nightfall, weak, mournful, distant signs of life were heard coming from the depths of the earth. Work was halted; emotion made breathing difficult. The astonished mother listened until convinced that there was a reply from within the mine, and then a delirious peal of triumphant laughter burst from her lips.

"There he is! He's calling me! He's saying, 'Oh, Mama!' My precious, my darling! Don't die, my love! Your mama's going to get you out, my joy! Wait, my son, wait! Now, you're going to get out now!"

On her knees, she tried to kiss the rescuers' hands. The closest one was Ramón Luis; a burning mouth and flaming tears touched him. The miner jumped backwards. 'The bastard was alive? Was there no justice?' Nevertheless, he grabbed his shovel.

"Dig, dig!" repeated Juaneca, dancing with a frightening joy. "Dig, my friends!"

They dug and dug, excited, their efforts redoubled by hope and by the groaning that was more perceptible with each passing hour. Like the strapping youth that he was, Ramón Luis shoveled in an arrogant fit of energy, and he alone advanced more than three of the others. He thought there was hatred in his heart when really there was an infinite desire, a victorious one now, to tunnel into the wall and free the trapped miners. 'As soon as he comes out, I'll break his head apart with the shovel.' And he kept digging, tirelessly, furiously. The engineer praised him and singled him out as an example to the others, urging them on.

"Don't you hear them in there calling for help? I hear them as clear as a bell. Come on!"

Hoes, shovels, and pickaxes flew in a whirlwind of activity. The agonizing appeal for help could now be heard as if the trapped men were issuing it right alongside the diggers. They all wanted to be the first ones in making the hole and seeing the faces of the walled in men. It was Ramón Luis who accomplished it. At the opening cut by his powerful shovel, the face of a specter appeared, a face of a dying man in agony; the mother jumped up, moved Ramón Luis away, and planted her lips on her son's squalid face, babbling and raving in a joyful outburst.

A half hour later the rescue was concluded. The extricated miners, almost lifeless, were transported on stretchers to the improvised hospital, where they were attended with great care. Ramón Luis watched the procession of stretchers move off, and searched within himself for fury, rage, and a desire for death, amazed at not finding them.

Where were they? Why had they deserted him? His "obligation," his "obligation" was not to stop until finding them . . . Straightening his shoulders, he set out on the road home. He needed to wash, eat, sleep . . . What the hell, the body isn't made of iron!

The Broken Windowpane

There exist beings who are superior or at least different and even resistant to the environment into which they're born. One of these beings was Goros Aguillán, protagonist of the true and insignificant tale that was related to me in the village, where people discuss it without understanding it very much and attribute to it one absurd explanation after another.

Goros was the eldest of the five or six children of a peasant sacristan, a man as lazy as a snail and as poor as a church mouse. There not being a single red cent in the house, nor the inclination to earn one by working, one can imagine their state of abandonment; dwelling and inhabitants alike were squalid and filthy. The home of the Aguillán family was, however, one of the most spacious and well-built in the hamlet, but negligence and slovenliness had transformed it into a revolting pigpen. From the time that Goros—Gregorio—was old enough to grip a broom, the handle of which he fashioned from gorse and the brush from field myrtle, he devoted himself on Sundays, with the ardor of a calling that is revealed, to sweeping, cleaning, tidying up, and leaving everything spotless. The neighbors made fun of him, his mother gave him a nickname . . . and he kept sweeping, redoubling his efforts, feeling himself in a world apart, a superior one, far away from his class of people, inside a more noble and refined existence which he didn't recognize but presaged with a kind of intuition; and the only example of this existence that had appeared before his eyes was the country manor of the gentry with its wide, silent, dignified salons and light-colored windows. Speaking of which, Goros suffered a daily torment on seeing in the dilapidated window of the little room, where he and four younger brothers and sisters slept crowded together, a broken pane, consisting of little more than jagged, dusty fragments stuck to the frame, and held in place by means of an oily piece of paper that had been pasted over it. If Goros had had money . . . ! Every

137

morning, upon awakening, the sight of the shabby repair of the plate of glass triggered in him the same feeling of rage. He said nothing. What for? His father would have responded that such was the condition of the windowpanes throughout the parish; his mother, more quick-tempered, would have cuffed him on the back of the neck; and as for his siblings, they would look at him dumbfounded—like the ducks and hens in the pond and muddy yard, they romped happily in the filth.

At the age of fifteen, Goros, acting upon what he had been planning, managed, illegally or as a stowaway, to slip aboard an ocean liner that was departing Marineda for South America. He was beginning to build his own world, fleeing that unwholesome hole—naturally the play on words wouldn't have occurred to him—in which Fate had confined him.* And the fact is that on losing sight of the coast, on distinguishing in the distance what looked like a faint red sparkling that was dying out, the flashing of Marineda's glassed-in balconies, he felt a sudden dull pain, a stab in the heart, which was love for what he was leaving even while detesting it. An incongruity in our makeup, foam from the sea of contradictions in which we swim!

The feeling of affection for what he left behind became more pronounced with time. Goros, after cruel hardships and back-breaking jobs, was beginning to hold his own. When he gained a solid footing, he prospered quickly. His business acumen, his instinct for modern comforts earned him the esteem of his employers; once a partner in the firm, he effected its amazing upsurge. Wealth, which he desired only to satisfy certain artistic pretensions of enjoyment in the art of others, because he would never be a creative artist, flowed into his hands. It would be more unlikely for it to flow into those of artists! And one morning Goros awoke on his way to becoming a millionaire, seeing the future through clear, wide lenses without a speck of dust on them.

More than ever he remembered the old house of the Aguillán family, and the ugly windowpane, broken and covered with greasy paper that was pushed back and forth by drafts and darkened by swarming, buzzing clouds of flies . . . A number of times he had sent money orders in regular amounts to free his brother from conscription, to defray the costs of his mother's serious illness, and to pay for the wedding of his little sister, who started a business by opening a shop in Areal.* It was a steady drain; every mail delivery brought a painful, mournful entreaty, a cry of dire straits. Goros now reflected that he was in a position to advance money without waiting for them to implore him humbly. And he generously wired a nice little sum: six thousand *pesos* in gold, for the hereditary home to be repaired, restored, furnished, and put in order decorously and without delay. "Have them put very strong and very attractive panes in the windows; have them change that broken one, and let the servant, because it's essential for my mother to have a servant in her employ, wash them every now and then. I highly recommend this. In dirty windowpanes is the source of a thousand illnesses, I warn you." And after Goros, who was now Don Gregorio, wrote this paragraph, he experienced a sweet, inner sense of satisfaction, picturing the venerable mansion, so squalid before and today a source of amazement in the village—it would be painted, whitewashed, and its windows would gleam in the sun; there would be an orchard-garden, tended by day laborers without his ailing father having to stoop to break up clods . . .

When such images spring to mind, they occasion an irresistible temptation to want to contrast them with reality. With his travels increasingly more brief and easy and with his business ventures well under way, Don Gregorio decided to visit his village unannounced—it's the predictable pattern of every *indiano*.* And what he thought of doing was what he did. He disembarked at Marineda, where nobody knew him, and hired the first coach that he saw hitched at the foot of the wharf; he loaded on it only his splendid traveling bag and, in a voice that quavered a little, ordered: "To Santa Morna." He himself wouldn't have known how to express what blunted his spirit. If he had managed to cry, he would've felt completely happy. He was thinking, more than about his family, about the house, the dwelling place. What excitement to find the decrepit, gloomy mansion alive and rejuvenated! And he offered the coachman a tip to make haste.

On sighting the dreamed-of place he doubted his eyes . . . because faith has this rare virtue: we believe that it is *what it ought to be* and disbelieve the evidence. There stood the house, right there, but no different than the one Don Gregorio had left upon departing: the same pile of manure at the door, the same foul puddle that rains had saturated with the fetid purée of the dunghill, the selfsame rotten unpainted doors, the selfsame façade of earth and slate, where pellitories grew . . . Good God, is this possible?

He rushed headlong inside . . . Instead of embracing them, he asked them for an explanation. The father, trembling, was almost on his knees before that wealthy gentleman who was his son.

"San Amaro help us! Goros . . ., my dear boy . . ., it was one of those things . . . No harm intended . . . We bought land, thank goodness, with the welcome money that you sent . . . The house, it's good enough for us; may God give us another like it in heaven."

"You can go up," added the mother, triumphantly, "and you'll notice that we changed the pane in the window, as you instructed . . ."

Don Gregorio hurried to his miserable little room where childhood dreams fluttered back and forth. It was true; in place of the broken windowpane, a new one—greenish and smeared with putty—had been installed. Don Gregorio didn't realize what was happening to him, what mental turmoil he was feeling. That windowpane! In spite of the filth and dirt that he no longer remembered, how many times had he looked at it upon awakening, blinking his eyes in the sun that made fun of him? Fresh air and the smell of the countryside used to reach him through that windowpane, and even the flies on it were priceless, and even the edges shone occasionally. And turning sadly to his mother, he murmured:

"It wasn't meant to be! Remove the windowpane!"

And in the village of Santa Morna they don't know why the *indiano* left so crestfallen and downcast, when his mother, as she's fond of saying, had indulged him in almost everything.

The White Hair

My Aunt Elodia had written affectionately: "Come and spend Christmas with me. I'll have sweets that you like." So after my father gave me his permission and something even more important, the money to make the short trip, I journeyed to Estela* by coach. At dusk I got out on the small square surrounded by venerable buildings, at the inn's unusual carriage entrance.

At first, I considered going straight to my aunt's home; then, on one of those impulses that nobody takes the trouble to think through—we find the reasons to be so insignificant—I decided not to put in an appearance until the following day. I knew that my aunt's house at that hour would be like a dark and boring little cave; I also pictured the commotion if I did go. Her only maid, shuffling and shielding a small oil lamp with her hand, would come out to unlock the door. My Aunt Elodia would fret about having to add a meat dish to supper; she assumed that all single young men were carnivorous creatures. And she would ask for an explanation, like why hadn't I given advance warning. Keys would squeak and clink, sheets would have to be brought out for me . . . And it was, above all, a night to be free! A young man, for as levelheaded as he may be, who comes from the country, from an ancestral manor house where he spent the fall alone with his parents, is attracted to freedom.

I left my valise at the inn and, wrapped in my cape because it was getting cold, fell to wandering about the streets, taking a special pleasure in it. Under the first few sections of the old arcade, I ran into a former classmate, one of those whom we call friends because we had some good times and laughs together, even if they're different from us in character and upbringing. For the same reason that I found it amusing to stroll through freezing and empty streets—the long stretch of country living—I was prompted to greet Laureano Cabrera with a truly cordial expansiveness. I explained to him the reason for my trip and invited

141

him to have supper with me. After he accepted, I noticed, in the light of a street lamp, his sickly air and haggard appearance. Depravity had ravaged his body and penury showed in his castoff clothing. He looked like a beggar. And when he moved, he gave off a pronounced odor of stale tobacco, sweat, and urea. My observations were confirmed when he pleaded with me in an anguished tone of voice to lend him some money. He needed it, urgently, that very night. If he didn't get it, he was capable of shooting himself in the head.

"I can't help you," I replied. "My father didn't give me very much."

"Why don't you go and ask Doña Elodia for it?" he asked suddenly. "She has money stashed away."

I remember that all I said was: "I'd be embarrassed."

At that moment we were crossing under the direct light of another street lamp and Laureano's face appeared, brightly illuminated, as if it had sprung out of the darkness. Worn and debauched from excess, it retained, nevertheless, a stamp of intelligence, because long ago we all agreed that Laureano "showed promise." In the brief moment that I managed to get a good look at him, I noticed a change that surprised me: passage from a state that in him must been habitual—ingrained cynicism, the farce of sponging—to a sudden, inner resolve that hardened his facial features in a sinister manner. Almost as if something strange had just occurred to him.

'This one'll waylay me,' I thought, and out loud I suggested that we have supper, not at the questionable, brothel-like hovel that he recommended, but at the inn. A distrust, viscous and repulsive like a reptile, was creeping through my spirit, troubling it. I didn't want to be alone with such an individual, even if it struck me as unseemly to retract the invitation to eat.

"I'll wait for you there," I added. "At nine."

And I departed abruptly, shaking him off. The vague apprehension that had taken hold of me disappeared then. In order to avoid similar encounters, I raised the flap of my cape, pulled down my hat, and, turning off the central streets, headed for the house of a woman who had been my very good friend when I was studying law in Estela. I couldn't swear that I had thought about her three times since the days when I used to see her, but familiar places jog a person's memory and revive the senses, and that bend in the gloomy street, that rusty balcony, with flower-pots full of geraniums packed like sardines, took me back to the time when the devout Leocadia would secretly open the door for me, drawing back a well-oiled bolt. Because Leocadia, whom I met at a novena, was cautious and feline in everything, and her frequent devotions and modest bearing had made her highly esteemed in her close circle. Probably very few people suspected anything of our relationship, broken off simply because of my absence. Leocadia had a real husband over in the Philippines, an evil man, a rake who didn't always send every month the twenty-five *duros* with which she supported herself. And she would repeat to me over and over again:

"Don't be crazy. We have to be prudent. People are malicious. If somebody writes to him about rumors spread here . . ."

Recollection of these often repeated phrases caused me to adopt all sorts of precautions and go out of my way not to be seen when I climbed the narrow, shaky stairs. I knocked in the old, agreed-upon manner and Leocadia in person opened the door. She almost dropped the candle. I drew her inside and filled myself in. Nobody was there: the servant was a day maid and slept in her own home. But more caution than ever was needed because "you-know-who" had returned, laid off without pay because of some problems with the government, and fortunately he was in Marineda today trying to resolve the matter . . . In any event, the sooner I could leave, and as stealthily as possible, the better. Our Lady of Solitude! If he got wind of the slightest little thing!

Complying with her behest, I slipped away cautiously at a quarter to nine and threaded my way through the narrow, romantic streets toward the inn. As I was crossing in front of the cathedral, the clock struck with ominous pause and solemnity. Perhaps owing to the humidity, perhaps owing to the state of my nerves, I was startled by a violent chill. The prospect of the inn's thick, hot noodle soup and robust wine made me quicken my step. I had gone quite some time without eating.

Contrary to what I expected, since he wasn't known for his

punctuality, Laureano was already waiting for me, and had asked for his place setting and ordered supper. He greeted me with banter.

"Where have you been? You're quite the rascal, so it's anybody's guess."

In the yellowish but direct light of the oil lamps that hung from the ceiling, my friend's countenance horrified me even more, if that's conceivable. In the midst of the gaiety that he affected, and in his hastening to confess that shooting himself in the head was a joke and that he wasn't that hard-pressed, I detected something fiendish in his somber look and contorted mouth. Not knowing how to interpret the expression on his face, I assumed that he indeed was hounded by a suicidal impulse. I did notice, nevertheless, that he had dressed and spruced up a little. His hands were relatively clean, his necktie was knotted, and he had combed his matted hair. Across from us, a Catalan commission agent, a handsome, bearded young man, was already drinking his coffee and slowly sipping glasses of Martel while reading a newspaper. Inasmuch as Laureano raised his voice, the man ended up taking notice of us, and even smiled knowingly, partaking in Laureano's persistent jocularity.

"I'm still wondering where you were holed up. What a sly one! You haven't spent three hours pounding the streets. You can feed that line to someone else. Do you think I'm that gullible? As if anybody trusted these returning country boys."

The cautious Leocadia's entreaties were still buzzing in my ears and I considered myself duty-bound to maintain that, yes, I had spent the time walking the streets and wandering.

"And you," I retorted. "Praying the rosary, were you?"

"Me, I was at home!"

"Well, now. A home and all?"

"Yes. It's not a mansion, but it is a place to sleep. Braulia's boardinghouse. Don't you remember it?"

I remembered perfectly well. It was a foul, squalid, fourth-rate rooming house very close to where my Aunt Elodia lived. And at the very moment that I was remembering this particular, my eyes singled out, hanging from a button on Laureano's shabby coat, a glittering thread. It was a long, shiny, white hair.

You may or may not believe me. My reaction was violent, and profound; it'd be difficult for me to explain because I believe that there are a great many things beyond all rational analysis. Fascinated by the splendor of the silvery thread on the dirty old cloth, I didn't move, I didn't utter a sound: I kept quiet. Occasionally I wonder what would have happened if I had been moved to tease him about it. But the fact is that I didn't say a word. It was as if I had been bewitched. I couldn't take my eyes off that white hair.

At the end of supper Laureano's good humor faded, and when coffee was served, he was sullen and ill at ease; he glanced frequently toward the door and his hands were trembling so much that he broke a brandy glass. Some time had gone by since the Catalan left us alone in the gloomy dining room sitting in front of earthenware toothpick holders shaped like tomatoes and blue vases with dusty, artificial flowers, The waiter, in search of his own supper, was probably in the kitchen. Cabrera, more somber by the minute, was jittery and wary, emptying glass after glass of cognac, and talking hurriedly about inconsequential matters or lapsing into spells of silence. There came a moment in which he must have thought, 'I'm on the verge of being completely drunk,' and stood up, a little shaky in the legs as well as speech.

"So you're not coming back there with me, huh?"

I knew only too well what there was, and the mere thought of it in such company and of going out in the torrential downpour that had begun to fall . . . No! To my inviting bed to sleep peacefully until the following day, and not see Cabrera again. I put his cape around his shoulders, handed him his greasy hat, and said goodbye to him.

"Goodnight. Don't mention it. Enjoy yourself, Laureano!"

I fell into a deep sleep which was disturbed by formless nightmares of the kind that aren't remembered upon awakening. And I was awakened by a racket at the door: the owner of the inn in person, terrified, came in followed by a police inspector and two agents.

"You, sir! They've come for you. You're to get dressed!"

At first I didn't understand. The inspector's gruff, deliberately ambiguous phrases enabled me to grasp only part of the truth.

Later, hours later, in front of the judge, I learned all that needed to be known. My Aunt Elodia had been strangled and robbed the night before, and I was being accused of the crime.

The most peculiar thing was that the awful occurrence didn't surprise me! You could say that I was expecting it. Something like it had to happen. Someone, perhaps the very spirit of my dead aunt, had apprised me of it indirectly. Except that now was when I understood, now when I was unraveling the black foreboding.

The judge, grim and concerned, received me with a mixture of sternness and politeness. I was "such a respectable" person that they weren't going to treat me like a common criminal. I was given an explanation of why I was under suspicion and told that they were waiting for my deposition before they changed detention to imprisonment. I needed to exonerate myself, because if not, what with the newspapers and the uproar that had broken out in the town, for as willing as the judge was. . . We had better get to it. First the facts without the trappings of an interrogation, more like a confidential chat. I should've gone to spend the night at my aunt's house. My bed there was made. Why, then, did I sleep at the inn?

"Just one of those things . . . So as not to disturb my aunt at an inconvenient hour."

Not disturb? Careful now, I was to pay close attention. These were, according to the judge, the facts. I had gone to Doña Elodia's house around seven o'clock. The maid, who is stonedeaf, didn't want to unlock the door. From the peephole I shouted, "It's her nephew," and then my aunt came to the anteroom and instructed her to let me in. I entered the living room and the maid went off to make supper, because she had been told what to do in case I arrived. From that point until nine or a little after, nobody knows what happened. When it was ready, the maid came in to announce supper and saw that there was nobody in the room and that everything was in darkness. She called out several times; nobody answered. Frightened, she lighted a lamp. Her mistress's bedroom was locked. Then, shaking from fear, the only thing she managed to do was lock herself in too, in her room. At daybreak she went down to the street and consulted the neighbor women; two or three of them went back up with her and she called out again, shouting to her mistress. Finally, the authorities forced the lock. The victim lay on the floor under a mattress. At one corner a stiff foot showed. The closet, forced open and ransacked, displayed its contents. Two chairs had fallen.

"My conscience is clear," I exclaimed. "The maid must have seen that man's face."

"She says that she didn't. He had his cape wrapped around him and his hat pulled way down. She didn't see him. And she's so dense, so foolish, so timid. The woman's somewhat dazed."

"Then I'm lost, I declared.

"Calm down. It's true there are many coincidences. You arrived yesterday at six. At six-fifteen you talked to a friend on Bebederos Street. Then, until nine, nothing more is known about you. At nine you have supper at the inn with the same friend, and a commission agent who was there has testified that the question "where had you spent those hours" upset you, and he also says that you claimed you had spent them walking the streets, which is improbable. It rained cats and dogs from eight until eight-thirty and you didn't have an umbrella. He also said that you were kind of . . . like worried at times, and the waiter says that you broke a glass. It's a stroke of bad luck!"

"Has the one who had supper with me testified?"

"Yes, he has. That useless Cabrera has testified. Pretty much what we knew. That he saw you, beforehand, for a short time; that you invited him to supper; that he went; and that around eleven he left."

"He's the one who killed my aunt!" I cried out firmly. "He's the one. Nobody else."

"But that's not possible! He related to me everything that he did. During those hours he was in his lodging house."

"No, sir. I say he went in, made sure he was seen, and left again. In that kind of flophouse the door's never locked. There isn't anybody to keep watch. He knew that my Aunt Elodia was expecting me. He's clever. He set it up cunningly. Laureano's really down-and-out. When he ran into me on Bebederos Street he asked me for money, threatening to blow his brains out if I didn't give it to him. Now it's all clear: I see it as if it were happening in front of me."

"What you say is worthy of consideration. However, I must

warn you that your position is precarious. As long as you can't account for your movements between six and nine."

My blood ran cold. I must have been white, with purple rings under my eyes. I was up against one of those what's-your-alibi judges who hold firm. Alibi? It would be a foul, despicable act to involve Leocadia—every woman has the honor that befits her—and besides, it would be futile, because I know her . . . she's no theatrical or fictional heroine and would deny everything I said. And I'd deserve it. I wasn't a murderer, or a thief, but . . .

Remorse gripped my heart, squeezing it in its iron grasp. I thought I felt my blood oozing out . . . It was salty tears in the corners of my eyes. And at that very instant, a flash! I remembered the shiny thread tangled on the button of the threadbare coat.

"Your Honor . . ."

The white hair was still there when they ordered the criminal to appear in court. Aunt Elodia's moneybag was found hidden in his straw mattress, along with the key to her bedroom. Nevertheless, there are some, even today, who say that the entire affair was suspect, that maybe I turned in my own accomplice. And a good name—I no longer have one. There is an ineradicable shadow in my life. I've gone into seclusion in the village, and when Christmas draws near, for weeks at a time I don't get out of bed, to avoid seeing people.

Don Carmelo's Salvation

Those of us who knew the priest from Morais were a little scandalized that he remained in charge of his parish. And in fact, confirming our astonishment, which verged on indignation, it didn't take long for him to be assigned a coadjutor *in capite,** and he ended up somewhat like a reserve soldier, prevented from committing further outrages during his ministry.

Don Carmelo was a disaster. When going to the fairs and village feast days that he always attended on horseback, perhaps he didn't risk loss of balance atop his nag's back, but on the return leg it seemed truly miraculous that he stayed in the ramshackle saddle because gravity is, supposedly, an imperative natural law, and the priest would lean excessively from one side to the other. Rumor has it that one time he rolled into the ditch. He didn't hurt himself. There are states in which the body turns rubbery. Bacchus doesn't usually travel alone at these rural solemnities and gatherings; grimy playing cards keep him company, and Don Carmelo was capable of gambling away even his clerical collar and biretta. He was so impoverished and in debt that at times he literally had nothing for food, although it's claimed that he never ran short for drinks.

As if these traits were insufficient, accounts go on to state that Don Carmelo was more than quarrelsome. Wherever a row started, there was the priest from Morais, his face flushed a deep purple, his eyes flashing angrily and his fist raised to thrash mercilessly, asserting himself with the most ostentatious bravado, because wherever he was no bully held sway, and when Don Carmelo's blood boiled it was better to leave him alone.

With regard to other weaknesses that reveal the miserable side of the human condition, much discussion took place, and there were supporters of the priest who maintained that in this respect he hadn't committed any grievous offenses; but those who denounced him in the very same respect had a powerful argument

the day they saw at Don Carmelo's house a baby boy, a lovely
one to be sure, only days old, whom the priest and his boorish
housekeeper raised as best they could, with the old woman feeding him cow's milk and cornmeal porridge.

The child endured this regimen and even the sips of wine that
Don Carmelo dispensed to comfort him in his tantrums, and he
grew up strong, mischievous, good-looking and curly-headed like
a frizzy mountain bush, continuously feeding the gossip mill
because nobody knew who his parents were.

"So then, this youngster, you found him behind a shrub, is that
it?" he was asked slyly by the archpriest of Loiro, a very influential man in the diocesan clergy.

And Don Carmelo, who saw what was coming, answered
abruptly:

"Something like that. I was returning from Estela, at the time
of the retreat the archbishop foisted on us, would that he had to
take his own medicine . . . I know what a . . . and as sure as God
is listening to us, I was smoking as I rode, absorbed in other
things, and if I was thinking at all, it was about how late it was
getting to reach home by suppertime. Besides, it was beginning
to rain, and my nag appeared none too anxious to get a move on;
he'd been in the stable so long that you could tell he had still
joints. Anyway, I was digging in my heels to hurry him along,
when I think to myself: 'If I had a little green switch this rascal
wouldn't make fun of me.' And there to the left of the highway I
see some willows, and I jump down to cut a switch with my
knife, when I hear the crying of a little baby. I look all over, and
there was the youngster, wrapped in so many clothes, old rags
and colored shreds that his face wasn't visible. Again I looked
all over, thinking that perhaps his mother was around. I yelled.
Not a living soul responded. I rode for nearly a mile without
stopping, asking at all the houses with the bawling baby under
my arm, and nobody knew anything; everybody registered great
surprise. At one house they took pity on us and gave the snivel-
ing thing a cup of milk, and he drank it all up, little by little.
What was I to do? I carried the baby away and took him home
with me. Ramoniña tried to claw me. She said she was going to
dump him down the well . . . like the cat's litters . . . and now
she does without so he can eat to his heart's content. Life's

strange, isn't it? Some cutie (that's what Don Carmelo called loose women) who was inconvenienced by the baby dropped him off there to die, but God had other plans."

In spite of the detailed circumstances with which Don Carmelo authenticated his account, a wink from the archpriest at other clergymen would usually indicate that nobody pulled a fast one on him, and that a wily old fox isn't fooled.

Ramoniña herself, the housekeeper, who looked as if she were made of fat, didn't swallow his story of finding the baby. She considered him homebred. In the beginning Don Carmelo irately rejected the suspicions; afterwards his only reaction was to shrug his shoulders. The little baby boy, nevertheless, shouldered a large share of the blame in the archpriest's harsh decision when he assigned the coadjutor to the censured cleric.

Don Carmelo resigned himself. He no longer bothered to repeat the story of the green switch and the infant recently wrapped in rags. When Ramoniña taught Angel, which was the boy's name, to hypocritically call the priest *Uncle*, Don Carmelo used sinful language and shouted in a gruff voice:

"No, call me Father! In the end they're all going to tell you, damn them, that you're my son."

Angel believed it in good faith; with the greatest naturalness he said *My father*, without noticing, at first, the malicious snickers of his listeners. Nevertheless, children grow up, and even in villages they catch on and become sharp, especially if they're as quick as this one was. The first time that Angel detected the denigrating intention with which he was being asked about his papa—the boy was only twelve—he unloaded such a punch in the speaker's nose, a prissy young priest, that he left his teeth chattering and his face covered with blood.

And since Don Carmelo was becoming increasingly more addicted to drink and more penniless, the boy, believing that he fulfilled a duty even more sacred than that of gratitude, set to work to support him.

Nobody knows how he learned the carpenter's trade in addition to farm chores. With his daily wage, supplemented by working in the vegetable garden, he succeeded in freeing the rectory from destitution, and displaying an energy that Nature seemed to inspire in him, he combated the vice that with age had completely dominated Don Carmelo. He was aided by attacks of gout that confined the priest to an old leather armchair and prevented him from satisfying his chronic dipsomaniac's thirst at fairs and tabernacles. Ramoniña had died, of complications from obesity, and the new maid, a young girl as small as a mountain rabbit, obeyed Angel unquestioningly. No wine or any of its derivatives got into the house, in spite of Don Carmelo's anguished pleas.

"Girl, get me a little drink."

"No. You'll have to excuse me."

The priest experienced, as a result of this rigorous regimen, a remarkable improvement, to the point of feeling so well that, like someone who's fleeing from a jail, he escaped with thief-like precautions, saddled his nag, and went to the funeral of Don Antonio Vicente de la Lajosa, a prominent local gentleman and rich mayorazgo*. Naturally, after the religious ceremony, there was a huge meal, the funeral banquet at the ancestral home whose cellars were famous for their impressive volume and wine, the best in the region. And it flowed, let's not say in a torrent, but certainly in jugs filled to the brim, and Don Carmelo, happy in a way that he hadn't felt for some time, stuffed himself and staggered under the load of pig in abundance, chickens prepared in saffron, cod garnished with potatoes, and beef, also accompanied by potatoes, and seasoned with hot, spicy peppers. Because all these dishes are heavy and make the mouth drier than that of a dog at a run, they had to wash them down copiously with that blessed drink, still and cool in big casks, and which seemingly could not be consumed without every glass urgently calling for its companion, as if each successive one couldn't manage alone. The priest from Morais made up for his spare regimen to such an extent that he couldn't even join in a card game that was started up there. The wine and brandy served with coffee were his coup de grâce. Angel, who arrived in a desolate state, had to fetch him and take him, with the help of several neighbors and a lot of effort, back to the rectory. The following day the doctor let fly a number of expletives, which all boiled down to the fact that the priest wouldn't recover from his spree. He was bled and given enemas, to no avail. He died without regaining consciousness, while Angel, crying his heart out, refused to accept the reality of what had happened.

Here comes the supernatural aspect of the adventure. Some reporter must have interviewed St. Peter, because any other way it seems difficult to understand how all this was communicated to the living. The fact is that the poor priest from Morais appeared at the celestial gates, holding a little boy by the hand.

"You, here, you disaster?" grumbled St. Peter, who rattled hostilely his bunch of recently burnished keys.

"Sir, I . . . I recognize that it's bold of me."

"And you've come with the waif?"

"Yes, great Apostle . . . because I believe that here the truth is known and my colleagues' calumnies will not be repeated. Here I'll succeed in discovering who the no-good slut was that dumped this tyke near the brook to create a headache for me. It's a joke: all the bad things I did in my lifetime didn't cause me the trouble that this single good act did."

"Well, because of it you'll enter . . . if you weren't accompanied by this urchin, you wouldn't get past the gates."

The boy let go of the priest's hand and pushed him inside; he stayed outside, and in a chirpy voice exclaimed:

"Goodbye, Papa. See you later!"

Notes

Page references to this volume precede each note.

(21)   *The Pardon:* based on a real occurrence (statement by the author).

(21)   *Marineda:* Pardo Bazán's fictional name for La Coruña, her birthplace.

(23)   *king . . . princess:* Alfonso XII and María Cristina of Austria.

(25)   *baby:* the infanta (daughter of a king of Spain), María Mercedes, born in 1880.

(30)   *Cid: El Cid Campeador* [The Valiant Warrior]. Rodrigo Díaz de Vivar, ca. 1040–99, Spanish soldier and hero of the wars of reconquest against the Moors. His exploits are sung in *El Cantar de Mio Cid* [The Song of the Cid], an anonymous work of the twelfth century. Synonymous with a very brave person or champion of resistance.

(30)   *robbers:* bandits and marauding bands were a fact of life in Galicia (northwest Spain) throughout the nineteenth century. Pardo Bazán gives accounts of their gruesome brutality in her collection *Tales and Stories of Galicia,* one of which is "A Descendant of the Cid."

(30)   *fair of the fifteenth:* these market fairs were known in Galicia by the day of the month on which they were held.

(32)   *Lafuché:* Spanish deformation of the French *Lefaucheux,* a type of carbine.

(39)   *Godoy:* Manuel de Godoy (1767–1851), Spanish statesman and chief minister to Carlos IV from 1792 to 1808.

(39)   *Narváez:* Ramón María Narváez (1799–1868), Spanish general and politician who took up the cause of Isabel II against the Carlists.

(42)   *jaleo . . . cachucha:* popular Andalusian dances.

(43)   *duro:* the equivalent (today) of five *pesetas.*

(52)   *The Gravedigger:* the title in Spanish is *No lo invento* (*I'm not inventing* [*making*] *it* [*up*]).

(52)   *Puri la Casta:* Puri the Chaste. There is some redundance here since *Pura* can mean *chaste* as well as pure. *Puri* may come from *Purita* or [*María de la*] *Purificación.*

(52)   *Helen:* (in Classical mythology) the beautiful daughter of Zeus and Leda; her abduction by Paris led to the Trojan War.

(54)   *Hamlet . . . Ophelia:* act 5, scenes 1 and 2.

(56)   *inamorato of Venice: Romeo and Juliet,* act 5, scene 3.

(58)   *Lucrecia:* after being raped by Sextus Tarquinius, son of Lucius Tarquinius, a Roman despot, Lucrecia commited suicide, and legend has it that her act precipitated the dynasty's downfall.

(60)   *Murillo's . . . Refitolera:* Bartolomé Esteban Murillo (1617–82), famous for his religious paintings and in particular for his Madonnas. *Refitolera* (woman in charge of a refectory) is one of his pictures.

(70) *Isis:* goddess of fertility in ancient Egypt. In statuary she was frequently represented with her head veiled, a symbol of mystery.

(73) *Ganymede:* (in Classical mythology), a Trojan youth, cupbearer of the gods.

(75) *Gospel:* This afterward was added later, when the story was published as part of a collection (*Tales Sacred and Profane*). Pardo Bazán was viciously attacked for this story by, amongst others, the Bishop of Madrid, Don José de Cos y Macho, because of its supposed doctrinal impurity and blasphemous view. It created a furor, in its intensity not unlike the controversy surrounding the recent film *The Last Temptation of Christ*, and the author found herself forced to defend her artistic right to produce works of imagination.

(77) *Haidée:* canto 2 of *Don Juan.*

(83) *A Galician Mother:* based on a real occurrence (statement by the author).

(83) The Salic Law introduced in Spain in 1713 by Felipe V of the Bourbon line excluded females from the throne. Although it was abrogated as the Pragmatic Sanction by the Cortes [Parliament] in 1789 at the request of Carlos IV, the change was never published nor printed in the collection of laws. The tyrannical Fernando VII, eldest son of Carlos IV, was childless after the death of his first three wives; he married his fourth, María Cristina, 12 December 1829. Several months later, in March of 1830, he decreed the royal Pragmatic Sanction so that Cristina's children, even if female, could succeed to the throne. After his death on 29 September 1833, his brother Carlos (to become known as the Pretender) contested Fernando's will, which provided for Cristina to rule as regent for their two-year-old daughter Isabel. The civil wars that ensued bore his name; the first Carlist War (the time period of "A Galician Mother") was fought between 1833 and 1840. Most of the action took place in the north of Spain. The Christinists were called Nationalists and were viewed as liberal, radical, and anticlerical, and enjoyed the support of most of the regular army; the Carlists were called Absolutists and Serviles and were viewed as conservatives and staunch defenders of the Church. In the hope of autonomy, the Basque provinces and Catalonia supported Carlos.

(97) *iron collar:* punishment that consisted of exposing criminals to public derision with their necks in an iron collar that was fastened to a post.

(104) *real:* monetary unit of the nineteenth century; a fourth part of the *peseta.*

(106) *Pactolus:* small river in ancient Lydia (Asia Minor), famous for the gold washed from its sands.

(111) The white horse in question is that of the apostle St. James the Greater, patron saint of Spain. In Spanish art he is frequently depicted— mounted on his white charger—leading Christians in battle against the Moors. This story is charged with symbolic overtones; it was first published on 28 August 1899, a year after the Spanish-American War, during which Spain lost Cuba, Puerto Rico, and the Philippines. The nation, many Spaniards believed, was mired in past glories and needed to forge a sense of national purpose.

(111) *Boabdil:* last Moorish king of Granada, late fifteenth century.

(112) *yellow and red:* the colors of the Spanish flag.

(112) *Boanerges:* a surname given by Jesus to James and John (see Mark 3:17).
(113) *St. Isidore:* San Isidro, a husbandman who worked as a farm laborer and is patron saint of the city of Madrid (not to be confused with San Isidoro, Archbishop of Seville).
(120) *The Lady Bandit:* based on a real-life figure.
(138) *He . . . him:* the first part of the sentence is a play on the word *mundo:* Empezaba a realizar su *mundo* propio, huyendo de aquel *mundo in-mundo* (*mundo,* world; *inmundo,* filthy, foul, squalid).
(139) *Areal:* Pardo Bazán's fictional name for Sada, on the coast, not far (east) of La Coruña.
(139) *indiano:* A Spanish emigrant who returns rich from Latin America.
(141) *Estela:* Pardo Bazán's fictional name for Santiago de Compostela, cultural capital of Galicia.
(149) *in capite:* (Lat.) at the head, i.e. in charge.
(152) *mayorazgo:* the eldest son and heir to an entailed estate under primogeniture.

Original Titles

El indulto/The Pardon
Nieto del Cid/A Descendant of the Cid
El premio gordo/First Prize
En tranvía/On the Streetcar
No lo invento/The Gravedigger
La última ilusión de don Juan/Don Juan's Last Illusion
La culpable/The Guilty Woman
La novia fiel/The Faithful Fiancée
La sed de Cristo/Christ's Thirst
Voz de la sangre/Blood Bond
La visión de los Reyes Magos/The Vision of the Three Magi
Madre gallega/A Galician Mother
Los huevos pasados/Soft-Boiled Eggs
El encaje roto/The Torn Lace
La lógica/Logic
Sustitución/The Substitute
Desde allá/From the Beyond
Consuelo/Consolation
El caballo blanco/The White Horse
Las tijeras/Scissors
La capitana/The Lady Bandit
La enfermera/The Nurse
El gemelo/The Cuff Link
Salvamento/Rescue
El vidrio roto/The Broken Windowpane
La cana/The White Hair
La salvación de don Carmelo/Don Carmelo's Salvation

Select Bibliography

English Translations of Pardo Bazán's Novels

A Christian Woman [Una cristiana]. Trans. Mary Springer. New York: Cassell, 1891.

Homesickness [Morriña]. Trans. Mary J. Serrano. New York: Cassell, 1891.

The Swan of Vilamorta [El cisne de Vilamorta]. Trans. Mary J. Serrano. New York: Cassell, 1891.

A Wedding Trip [Un viaje de novios]. Trans. Mary J. Serrano. New York: Cassell, 1891.

The Angular Stone [La piedra angular]. Trans. Mary J. Serrano. New York: Cassell, 1892.

The Mystery of the Lost Dauphin [Misterio]. Trans. Annabel Hord Seeger. New York and London: Funk & Wagnalls, 1906.

Midsummer Madness [Insolación]. Trans. Amparo Loring. Boston: Clark, 1907.

The Son of the Bondwoman [Los pazos de Ulloa]. Trans. Ethel H. Hearn. New York and London: Lane, 1908.

The House of Ulloa [Los pazos de Ulloa]. Trans. Paul O'Prey and Lucia Graves. London and New York: Penguin, 1990.

The House of Ulloa [Los Pazos de Ulloa]. Trans. Roser Caminals-Heath. Athens: University of Georgia Press, 1992.

English Translations of Pardo Bazán's Short Stories

NOT INCLUDED IN THIS VOLUME:

"First Love" ["Primer amor"]. In World's Great Romances. Anon. trans. New York: Black, 1929.

"Sister Aparición" ["Sor Aparición"]. In Spanish Stories and Tales. Trans. Harriet de Onís. New York: Knopf, 1954.

"The Revolver" ["El revólver"]. In Spanish Stories: Cuentos españoles. Trans. Angel Flores. New York: Bantam, 1960.

"The Heart Lover" ["Un destripador de antaño"]. In Great Spanish Short Stories. Trans. Edward and Elizabeth Huberman. New York: Dell, 1962.

"The Talisman" ["El talismán"]. In Classic Tales from Modern Spain. Trans. William E. Colford. Great Neck, NY: Barron's, 1964.

INCLUDED IN THIS VOLUME:

"The Pardon" ["El indulto"]. In Tales from the Italian and Spanish. Anon. trans. New York: Review of Reviews, 1920.

"A Churchman Militant" ["Nieto del Cid"]. In *Tales from the Italian and Spanish*. Anon. trans. New York: Review of Reviews, 1920.

"The Last Will of Don Javier" ["Desde allá"]. In *Tales from the Italian and Spanish*. Anon. trans. New York: Review of Reviews, 1920.

"First Prize" ["El premio gordo"]. In *Great Stories of All Nations*. Trans. Armando Zegri. New York: Brentano's, 1927.

Original Spanish Texts of Pardo Bazán's Short Stories

A. *Obras completas*. 44 tomos. Madrid: V. Prieto y compañía, 1891–1922. (T.5, *Cuentos de Marineda*, 1892; T.10, *Cuentos nuevos*, 1894; T.16, *Cuentos de amor*, 1898; T.17, *Cuentos sacroprofanos*, 1899; T.20, *Un destripador de antaño* [*Historias y cuentos regionales*], 1900; T.23, *En tranvía* [*Cuentos dramáticos*], 1901; T.25, *Cuentos de Navidad y Reyes, Cuentos de la patria, Cuentos antiguos*, 1902; T.31, *El fondo del alma* [*Cuentos del terruño*], 1907; T.36, *Sudexprés*, 1909; T.43, *Cuentos de la tierra*, 1922)

B. *Cuentos escogidos*. Valencia: P. Aguilar, 1891.

C. *Cuentos trágicos*. Madrid: Biblioteca Renacimiento, 1921.

D. *La dama joven y otros cuentos*. Barcelona: Biblioteca Arte y Letras, 1885.

E. *Nuevo Teatro Crítico*. 30 nos. Madrid: La España Editorial, 1891–1893; for "No lo invento" ["The Gravedigger"], no. 3, 1891.

F. *Obras completas*. 3 vols. 4th ed. Madrid: Aguilar, 1964–73. There are short stories in all three volumes.

G. Paredes Núñez, Juan. *Los cuentos de Emilia Pardo Bazán*. Granada: Imprenta de la Univ. de Granada, 1979. Excellent study which also contains an appendix (pp. 367–498) of twenty-seven (27) stories.

H. *Cuentos (Selección)*. Edición de Juan Paredes Núñez. Madrid: Taurus Ediciones, 1984. Very insightful introduction (pp. 9–72). Twenty-eight (28) stories.

I. *Cuentos y novelas de la tierra*. Selección, introducción, prólogos y notas por Marina Mayoral. 2 vols. Santiago de Compostela: Edicións Sálvora, 1984. A useful chronology and helpful prologue. Drawback: only titles of collections are given in the tables of contents, not the page numbers of individual stories; the only way to find them is to leaf through the volume. (1: *Cuentos del terruño, Historias y cuentos de Galicia, Cuentos de la tierra*; 2: *Cuentos de Marineda*.)

J. *Cuentos completos*. Edición de Juan Paredes Núñez. 4 vols. La Coruña: Fundación Pedro Barrié de la Maza, Conde de Fenosa, 1990 [a total of 1,961 pages]. Although the Introduction is taken almost verbatim from the opening pages of entry "G," above, this edition is a heroic effort. It will, I believe, supercede all previous collections of Doña Emilia's short stories and be the definitive text for some time to come because it contains 580 entries and a table of characters. In volume IV there is a chronology of the stories as well as an alphabetical listing by volume and page.

Secondary Sources in English

Boland, R. C. "The Antithesis between Religion and Nature in *Los Pazos de Ulloa*: A Different Perspective." *Revista Canadiense de Estudios Hispánicos*. 1981 Winter; 5(2): 209–215.

Bradford, Carole A. "The Treatment of Death and Rebirth in *La sirena negra*." *Revista Hispánica Moderna*. 1976–77; 39: 175–182.

Bretz, Mary Lee. "The Theater of Emilia Pardo Bazán and Concha Espina." *Estreno: Cuadernos del Teatro Español Contemporáneo*. 1984 Fall; 10(2): 43–45.

———. "Emilia Pardo Bazán on John Stuart Mill: Toward a Redefinition of the Essay." *Hispanic Journal*. 1988 Spring; 9(2): 81–88.

Brown, Donald F. *The Catholic Naturalism of Pardo Bazán*. Chapel Hill: University of North Carolina Press, 1957.

Charnon-Deutsch, Lou. "Naturalism in the Short Fiction of Emilia Pardo Bazán." *Hispanic Journal*. 1981 Fall; 3(1): 73–85.

———. *The Nineteenth Century Spanish Story: Textual Strategies of a Genre in Transition*. London: Tamesis, 1985.

DeCoster, Cyrus C. "Maupassant's *Une vie* and Pardo Bazán's *Los pazos de Ulloa*." *Hispania*. 1973; 56: 587–592.

———. "Pardo Bazán and Her Contemporaries." *Anales Galdosianos*. 1984; 19: 121–131.

Durham, Carolyn Richardson. "The Grotesque in the Short Stories of Emilia Pardo Bazán." *Dissertation Abstracts International*. 1987 Sept.; 48(3): 662A.

———. "Subversion in Two Short Stories by Emilia Pardo Bazán." *Letras Peninsulares*. 1989 Spring; 2(1): 55–64.

Feeny, Thomas. "Maupassant's 'Lui' and Pardo Bazán's 'La Calavera': A Possible Case of Influence." *South Atlantic Bulletin*. 1976; 41(iv): 44–47.

———. "The Child as Redeemer and Victim in Pardo Bazán's Short Fiction." *Revista de Estudios Hispánicos*. 1977; 11: 425–432.

———. "Pardo Bazán's Pessimistic View of Love as Revealed in *Cuentos de amor*." *Hispanófila*. 1978; 64: 7–14.

———. "Illusion and the Don Juan Theme in Pardo Bazán's *Cuentos de amor*." *Hispanic Journal*. 1980; 1(ii): 67–71.

Giles, Mary E. "Feminism and the Feminine in Emilia Pardo Bazán's Novels." *Hispania*. 1980; 63: 356–367.

Goldin, David. "Social and Psychological Determinants in *Morriña* by Pardo Bazán." *Crítica Hispánica*. 1981; 3(2): 133–139.

———. "The Metaphor of Original Sin: A Key to Pardo Bazán's Catholic Naturalism." *Philological Quarterly*. 1985 Winter; 64(1): 37–49.

González-Arias, Francisca. "Emilia Pardo Bazán and *La Tentation de Saint Antoine*, or the Countess and the Chimera." *Hispania*. 1988 May; 71(2): 212–216.

Hemingway, Maurice. *Emilia Pardo Bazán: The Making of a Novelist*. New York: Cambridge UP, 1983.

———. "Naturalism and Decadence in Zola's *La Faute de L'abbe Mouret* and Pardo Bazán's *La madre naturaleza*." *Revue de Littérature Comparée*. 1987 Jan.–Mar.; 61(1[241]): 31–46.

———. "Pardo Bazán and the Rival Claims of Religion and Art." *Bulletin of Hispanic Studies*. 1989 July; 66(3): 241–250.

Henn, David. *The Early Pardo Bazán: Theme and Narrative Technique in the Novels of 1879–89*. Liverpool: Cairns, 1988.

Mandrell, James. "Realism in Spain: Galdós, Pardo Bazán, Clarín and the European Context." *Neohelicon*. 1988; 15(2): 83–112.

Ordóñez, Elizabeth J. "'¿Mi niña?': Another Voice in *Los pazos de Ulloa*." *Discurso Literario*. 1985; 3(1): 121–131.

Pattison, Walter T. *Emilia Pardo Bazán*. New York: Twayne Publishers, 1971.

Quick, Ronald J. "The Cebre Cycle: Emilia Pardo Bazán and Galician Reform." *The American Hispanist*. 1977; 2(xviii): 10–11.

Rodríguez, Alfred; Velázquez, Socorro. "Incest in the Novels of Emilia Pardo Bazán." *Iris*. 1990: 89–97.

Sánchez, Porfirio. "How and Why Emilia Pardo Bazán Went from the Novel to the Short Story." *Romance Notes*. 1969; 11: 315–321.

Scanlon, Geraldine M. "Class and Gender in Pardo Bazán's *La tribuna*." *Bulletin of Hispanic Studies*. 1990 Apr.; 67(2): 137–150.

Schmidt, Ruth A. "A Woman's Place in the Sun: Feminism in *Insolación*." *Revista de Estudios Hispánicos*, 1974; 8: 69–81.

Tolliver, Joyce Lynn. "Pardo Bazán's Palimpsests: Narrative Perspective in Selected 'Love Stories.'" *Dissertation Abstracts International*. 1988 Jan.; 48(7): 1788A.

———. "Knowledge, Desire and Syntactic Empathy in Pardo Bazán's 'La novia fiel.'" *Hispania*. 1989 Dec.; 72(4): 909–918.

Vázquez, Mary S. "Class, Gender and Parody in Pardo Bazán's *La tribuna*." 679–687 in Fernández Jiménez, Juan et al, eds. *Estudios en homenaje a Enrique Ruiz-Fornells*. Erie, PA: Asociación de Licenciados y Doctores Españoles en Estados Unidos; 1990.

Whitaker, Daniel S. "The Power of Persuasion in Pardo Bazán's *La tribuna*." *Hispanic Journal*. 1988 Spring; 9(2): 71–80.

———. "Artificial Order: Closure in Pardo Bazán's *Insolación*." *Romance Quarterly*. 1988 Aug.; 35(3): 359–365.

Wood, Jennifer J. "Images of Feminine Evil in Emilia Pardo Bazán's *La quimera*." *Romance Quarterly*. 1990 Aug.; 37(3): 337–343.

Secondary Sources in Spanish, Galician, and French

Baquero Goyanes, Mariano. *El cuento español en el siglo XIX*. Madrid: C.S.I.C., 1949.

Barro, Teresa. "Misoxinia e feminismo." *Festa da palabra*. 1989 Fall; 6: 45–46.

Blanco Corujo, Oliva. "Emilia Pardo Bazán e a cuestión académica." *Festa da palabra*. 1989 Fall; 6: 72–74.

Bravo-Villasante, Carmen. *Vida y obra de Emilia Pardo Bazán*. Madrid: Ed. Magisterio Español, 1973.

Cannon, Harold L. "El esperpentismo en los cuentos de Emilia Pardo Bazán." *Káñina*. 1980 July–Dec.; 4(2): 61–65.

———. "Algunos aspectos estilísticos en los cuentos de Emilia Pardo Bazán." *Káñina*. 1983 July–Dec.; 7(2): 83–92.

Clémessy, Nelly. *Emilia Pardo Bazán como novelista: De la teoría a la práctica*. Madrid: Fundación Univ. Española, 1981.

Colmeiro, José F. "Relectura de la novela policiaca: *La gota de sangre* de Emilia Pardo Bazán." *Hispanic Journal*. 1989 Spring; 10(2): 33–48.

Cook, Teresa. *El feminismo en la novela de la Condesa de Pardo Bazán.* La Coruña: Diputación Provincial, 1976.

———. "Emilia Pardo Bazán y la educación como elemento primordial en la liberación de la mujer." *Hispania.* 1977; 60: 259–265.

Engler, Kay. "Estructura, diseño y sentido en *Morriña.*" *Explicación de Textos Literarios.* 1982; 10(2): 33–51.

Feal Deibe, Carlos. "La voz femenina en *Los pazos de Ulloa.*" *Hispania.* 1987 May; 70(2): 214–221.

García Negro, María Pilar. "Pardo Bazán: Feminismo, espíritu de clase, moralismo." *Festa da palabra.* 1989 Fall; 6: 56–69.

González-Arias, Francisca. "*La tribuna* de Emilia Pardo Bazán como novela histórica." *Anales Galdosianos.* 1984; 19: 133–140.

González Herrán, José Manuel. "Emilia Pardo Bazán y el naturalismo." *Insula.* 1989 Oct.; 44(514): 17–18.

———. "Zola y Pardo Bazán: De *Les Romanciers naturalistes* a *La cuestión palpitante.*" *Letras Peninsulares.* 1989 Spring; 2(1): 31–43.

González López, Emilio. *Emilia Pardo Bazán: Novelista de Galicia.* New York: Hispanic Institute, 1944.

González Torres, Rafael. *Los cuentos de Emilia Pardo Bazán.* Boston: Florentia, 1977.

Hermida, Carme. "Emilia Pardo Bazán e o rexurdimento." *Festa da palabra.* 1989 Fall; 6: 17–23.

Herrero Figueroa, Araceli. "Emilia Pardo Bazán, Crítica de Rosalía." II: 363–372 in *Actas do Congreso Internacional de Estudos sobre Rosalía de Castro e o Seu Tempo, II & III.* Santiago de Compostela: Consello da Cultura Galega, Univ. de Santiago de Compostela; 1986.

López, Mariano. "Los escritores de la Restauración y las polémicas literarias del siglo XIX en España." *Bulletin Hispanique.* 1979; 81: 51–74.

———. "Eclecticismo y evolución en la obra de Emilia Pardo Bazán." *Cuadernos Americanos.* 1981; 234(1): 46–63.

———. "El naturalismo transcendido de Emilia Pardo Bazán en *Un viaje de novios.*" *Letras Femeninas.* 1988 Spring–Fall; 14(1–2): 41–51.

Mayoral, Marina. "Emilia Pardo Bazán: 'Pena de muerte.'" 279–292 in *El comentario de textos, 3.* Madrid: Ed. Castalia, 1984.

———. "Emilia Pardo Bazán ante a moral sexual do seu tempo." *Festa da Palabra.* 1989 Fall; 6: 37–39.

Mouriz Barja, Isabel. "Algunhas mulleres dos contos e novelas." *Festa da palabra.* 1989 Fall; 6: 26–36.

Noia, Camino. "Aspectos feministas do pensamento da Pardo Bazán." *Festa da palabra.* 1989 Fall; 6: 47–55.

Osborne, Robert E. *Emilia Pardo Bazán: su vida y sus obras.* México, D.F.: Ediciones de Andrea, 1964.

Otero Cepeda, Encarna. "A fábrica de tabacos da Coruña." *Festa da palaba.* 1989 Fall; 6: 24–25.

Panero Menor, M. Carmen. "A luz das cartas de amor de doña Emilia Pardo Bazán." *Festa da palabra.* 1989 Fall; 6: 40–44.

Paredes Núñez, Juan. *Los cuentos de Emilia Pardo Bazán.* Granada: Imprenta de la Univ. de Granada, 1979.

———. *La realidad gallega en los cuentos de Emilia Pardo Bazán (1851–1921).* A Coruña: Ediciós do Castro, 1983.

———. "Maupassant en Espagne: D'une influence concrète du *Horla.*" *Revue de Littérature Comparée.* 1985 July–Sept.; 59(3)[235]): 267–279.

Porrúa, María del Carmen. "Una lectura feminista de *La tribuna* de Pardo Bazán." *Nueva Revista de Filología Hispánica.* 1989; 37(1): 203–219.

Rey, Alfonso. "El cuento sicológico en Pardo Bazán." *Hispanófila.* 1977; 59: 19–30.

Río Conde, Elisa "Breve estudio compartivo: Amparo y Tristana, mujeres del siglo XIX." *Letras de Deusto.* 1988 Jan.–Apr.; 18(40): 219–229.

Río Oliete, Mª. José del. "Pardo Bazán e a educación." *Festa da palabra.* 1989 Fall; 6: 70–71.

Rodríguez, Alfred; Fernández, Rosa. "La función de lo cinegético en *Los pazos de Ulloa. Iris.* 1988; 1: 61–68.

Santiáñez-Tío, Nil. "Una marquesita 'sandunguera' o el mito del naturalismo en *Insolación." Revista de Estudios Hispánicos.* 1989 May; 23(2): 119–134.

Scari, Robert M. "El cuento 'El destripador de antaño' de Emilia Pardo Bazán." *Revista de Literatura.* 1987 Jan.–June; 49(97): 169–180.

Vandivere, Julie. "Rebelión textual: A revolución feminista en *Los pazos de Ulloa." Festa da palabra.* 1989 Fall; 6: 6–16.

Varela Jácome, Benito. *Estructuras novelísticas de Emilia Pardo Bazán.* Santiago de Compostela: Instituto Padre Sarmiento, 1973.